Super Natural Simple

WHOLE-FOOD, VEGETARIAN RECIPES FOR REAL LIFE

Heidi Swanson

TEN SPEED PRESS
California | New York

Contents/

Super Natural Simple

A Short Note

These recipes stem from a busy time in my life. They have landed on these pages in the midst of a series of geographical moves, intensive projects, and, eventually, a pandemic.

I came to realize that this is actually the *only* time to write a book like this. When you're at your busiest (and feeling overwhelmed or overextended), cooking and eating well are usually the earliest casualties.

My hope is that you'll find plenty of delicious and doable recipes here to counter this tendency. This is a book for those times when it seems easier to grab something on the go or eat out or skip the meal entirely; the times when wholesome, nutrient-packed homemade meals are needed most.

Introduction

The cookbooks I love always have a strong sense of place, so if you'll indulge me a bit, I'll paint a picture of where this one originates. I'm writing from a small, sunny kitchen in a century-old Spanish bungalow. A bird's-eye view places me a block from an expansive stretch of beach running a few miles in length—from a neat-as-a-pin marina to a craggy jetty at the end of a long, dancer's leg of a peninsula. You can't go much farther south and still be in Los Angeles County. It's California, at volume ten.

At this moment, a glance through our south-facing windows reveals electric-red pomegranate flower blossoms and fiery banks of bougainvillea. From what I can tell, the plants here are happy, and I'm trying to get passion fruit, Arabian jasmine, kishu mandarins, makrut lime, and tiny rosella seedlings to take hold in a postage stamp–size space. There are herbs like tulsi and African basil, marjoram, yerba buena, and tangerine sage sprinkled about, and I water them with an old-fashioned metal watering can because I have yet to figure out the drip line.

I throw most of our meals together with ingredients I keep on hand. My goal is always to fix vibrant, nutrient-packed meals made primarily from whole, natural foods and I try to set up my kitchen to encourage and support that. When I open my pantry door, I see brown jasmine rice, dried mushrooms, chickpea pastas, tri-colored quinoa, fire-roasted tomatoes, and a rainbow of beans and lentils. Beyond that, seasonal vegetables set the tone for most meals, and I keep as many within eyesight as possible. This way, I'm more likely to integrate them into whatever I'm cooking.

California has enviable year-round farmers' markets, and Los Angeles has a great climate for maintaining a garden. For both, I'm exceptionally thankful. Intense, fresh, and bright flavors are what I crave and what inspire everything I cook. But if I'm being honest, my days are fuller than ever, and *this* detail, this busyness, is what defines my everyday cooking style as much as anything else. The more hectic my life becomes, the simpler my cooking has to be.

Simple is more of a feeling than anything else, and it's something I increasingly chase. A recipe that roasts for thirty minutes but only takes ten to get in the oven? Simple. Leveraging freezer items? Simple. A cake that comes together in one bowl? Yes, please. Generally speaking, balancing the idea of simple cooking while keeping things interesting is my sweet spot. I try to maintain efficiency in the kitchen without sacrificing flavor. When I'm cooking now, I'm most excited by recipes that are both succinct and special.

What you'll find here is a collection of whole-food, vegetarian recipes, all of which have been pared down for quick weeknight cooking via short ingredients lists, make-ahead techniques, and smart methods to create high-impact meals full of flavor, color, and nutrition. These are laid-back, crowd-pleasing power recipes rooted in plants, spices, color, nutrients, and flavor—the kinds of dishes that are manageable on a weeknight.

STAY CONNECTED TO WHAT YOU EAT

In 2007, I wrote *Super Natural Cooking*. It was a cookbook celebrating the power of natural foods at a time when cooking with whole grains and focusing on nutrient-dense plant-based ingredients wasn't as popular. *Super Natural Cooking* and its 2011 follow-up, *Super Natural Every Day*, highlighted a style of cooking and sourcing of ingredients that *felt right* to me. It made sense to eat real food and cook using mindfully grown, thoughtfully sourced ingredients. The case for vegetarianism (and veganism) was similar then to what it is now: better for the planet, better for the animals, better for our health and well-being.

In the years since, I've watched the coming and going of so many diet, eating, and cooking trends: Whole30, Atkins, low-carb, Paleo, Keto, turmeric-everything, warm lemon juice every morning, cupboards dedicated to

smoothie powders, extensive supplement and vitamin programs, and on and on. It's an intense and often overwhelming ecosystem, created by networked information culture, food politics, and diet wars colliding with people who are genuinely hoping to find their way to balance and good health. Unfortunately, many people end up ping-ponging from one trend and headline to the next.

When you cut through all of the claims and look at communities with the strongest longevity pockets, communities with elderly populations that experience a good quality of life well into their eighties and nineties, you find common threads. These folks tend to eat a 90 to 100 percent plant-based diet. And they build meals around greens, whole grains, beans, nuts, and tubers. So, while a lot of the information out there can be fun, inspiring, compelling, and, in many cases, helpful, finding your way to nutrient-rich, whole-food, plant-based meals is probably where you want to settle.

The trick, of course, is to identify and consistently integrate this type of cooking (and eating) into your life. My hope is that *Super Natural Simple* can step in here. If you are looking for approachable ways to work more vegetables and whole foods onto your plate, this book is for you. If you're looking for ways to phase out processed ingredients, restaurant meals, and take-out in place of super natural, weeknight-friendly meals, this book will help.

Natural foods and whole ingredients are wonderful, powerful, and often very beautiful. The magic (and benefits!) of integrating them into the rhythm of your life is real. Staying connected to what you eat is one of the most impactful ways to support your health and well-being. And modern life makes it so easy to disconnect with its bounty of prepared foods, restaurants, and delis.

The point of this book is to make you *want* to walk into your kitchen and cook healthful, wholesome meals. Even within the demands of modern life, regularly cooking for yourself can be transformational, and these recipes are definitely doable. Cooking and eating with others is one of the daily rituals that ties us together as human beings. If cooking hasn't previously been your thing, it's okay! It can be an adventure of sorts and an exciting world of deliciousness to explore. Experiment with new recipes a couple of times a week and, before you know it, you will have built a repertoire of go-to dishes you're excited about (see page 14).

When people ask me for advice about shifting to a more natural, plant-centric way of eating, there are a few key tips that I find myself expressing again and again. In practice, this advice comes together in a system of sorts, which I've outlined below. When you put these components in place, it's possible to create a positive ecosystem inside your own kitchen to help support you and your cooking aspirations.

1. Transition to natural ingredients.

2. Identify ten recipes you love.

3. Keep a well-stocked pantry.

4. "Merchandise" what you have.

5. Collect your equipment.

6. Use your freezer.

TRANSITION TO NATURAL INGREDIENTS

You see the term *natural* used a lot in marketing and packaging; it's a word that's often open to interpretation. That said, the spirit of the term *natural* is pretty straightforward. Natural ingredients are whole—they come straight from the plant or animal—or they are made from whole ingredients with as little processing as possible. For example, olives pressed into olive oil, almonds pureed into almond butter, tomatoes crushed into tomato sauce—these are natural foods. Foods that contain synthetic flavorings, stabilizers, and preservatives? Not natural. Natural foods tend to be packed with the good stuff: fiber, phytonutrients, protein, vitamins, and minerals. Ideally, they are the foundation of what you eat and what you cook with, most of the time. When you use natural ingredients, every meal is a fresh start, a new opportunity to power and nourish your body.

I won't call out every instance throughout the book because it can get repetitive, but I care about supporting farmers and producers who use

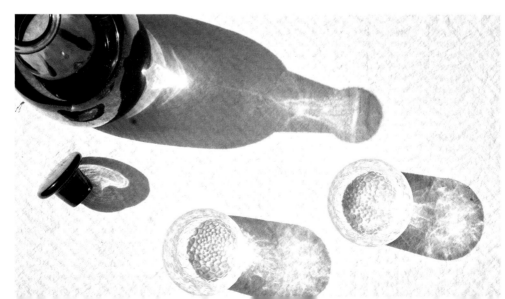

sustainable farming methods. Many of these are certified organic, and some of them aren't certified (for a whole host of reasons) but do farm using organic practices.

Hundreds of millions of pounds of pesticides and fungicides are sprayed on California fields each year. I even see them in use at my local community garden and on my block. This practice impacts the health of the people living and working nearby and our overall ecosystems. One way I vote for change is with my grocery dollars. Like many, I'm not perfect, and I don't always get it right, but supporting those who are trying to find their way out of the chemical haze helps ensure that we have a choice in the matter.

If you're currently cooking from an all-white pantry (white flour, white pasta, white sugar, white bread) or primarily eating prepared meals (meaning you have no connection to the cook or the ingredients), it's definitely possible to evolve over time. Getting other family members on board, figuring out what to cook and eat, and doing it in a way that works day to day can take a bit of figuring out. And patience! Maybe no one likes whole wheat rigatoni in your house, but soba noodles end up being a hit. Experimentation is key.

Start with some simple swaps. Switch from white rice to brown rice. Or sprinkle a handful of cooked quinoa, millet, or barley into your white rice. Replace your standard pasta with a whole grain or plant-based version. Introduce breads made with a percentage of whole grain or nut flours and dial up the percentage from there.

Equally important, eat the rainbow everyday by making sure you're getting plenty of green, red, purple, yellow, orange, and blue whole foods on your plate. It's easier if you keep big batches of vibrant, colorful snacks on hand, like the Pinkest Party Dip (page 66) or crunchy Puffed Rice Party Mix (page 63)—not just for parties! And having lots of quick-cooking vegetables like broccoli and cauliflower florets or asparagus spears to toss into pasta water or onto a roasting pan can boost every meal with little extra time or effort involved. You'll make thousands of food choices a year, so improving on even a small percentage of those adds up over time.

IDENTIFY TEN RECIPES YOU LOVE

Step two on your journey to eating more whole foods is to identify ten recipes that embody the way you aspire to cook and eat. There is *so* much food and recipe content out there, and it is easy to get overwhelmed. Creating a tight list of ten recipes helps you focus, shop, organize, and even delegate to other cooks in your household.

Your list might not come together overnight—it can take weeks or months, and that's okay—discovery is part of the fun, really. Build up the list over time, let it evolve, and make note of stand-out recipes that *really* work for you, your family, and your pace of life. These will become your go-tos. (Hopefully you'll find one or two here in this book!) Keeping the ingredients for these recipes on hand makes pulling your favorite meals together on a whim completely doable. Make a list of the core ingredients and save it on your phone, then pick them up each time you visit the store.

KEEP A WELL-STOCKED PANTRY

Having a full pantry of ingredient all-stars is one of the pillars of simple cooking. Good produce is the other. The recipes in this book use items that are readily available in just about any well-stocked grocery store; for example, Whole Foods Market and Trader Joe's. I mention a few wild cards that are fun to buy when you come across them—the sorts of ingredients I can't pass up or resist—but when these appear in recipes, I highlight them as optional.

If you have a well-stocked pantry, all you need for a great meal is some vibrant produce. I buy my fruits and vegetables from our local farmers' markets or let whatever looks good at the store dictate what ends up on our plates. Also, the recipes in this book are intentionally adaptable. If a recipe calls for broccoli but the in-season asparagus at the market looks great, by all means—make the swap!

YOUR SUPER NATURAL PANTRY

The following list is the foundation for most of the recipes in this book.

BEANS & PULSES. When you have these on hand, you're halfway to a finished meal. Keep a range of canned and dried beans and pulses at the ready. My go-to list includes chickpeas (garbanzos), French lentils (lentilles du Puy), black lentils, mung beans, cannellini beans, and quick-cooking red lentils. I also stock up on giant corona and gigante beans when I come across them.

BERRIES. When freeze-dried, the flavors of berries become concentrated, making them great additions to baked goods and homemade cereal blends. Look for fruit-only, unsweetened, unsulphured freeze-dried versions. I use them as the wild card ingredient in my favorite Big Raspberry-Rye Cookies (page 200).

CEREALS. Look for whole grain, unsweetened cereals to use in snacks, for baking, and for breakfast. Increasingly, there is a nice range of cereals available, for example: classic rolled oats, puffed millet, puffed kamut, and crisped brown rice.

CHEESES. If you want to avoid the animal rennet typically used in cheese making, there are more and more vegetable-rennet cheeses available, so keep your eyes peeled. New vegan cheese and other dairy products hit the market weekly, and many are worth trying.

CITRUS. I always have lemons and limes in my crisper drawer for fresh juice and zest. Big squeezes of citrus juice are my go-to way to add an acidic bite and balance to soups, pastas, salads, and dressings. I have a hard time passing up grapefruit, blood oranges, tangerines, kumquats, and mandarins as well.

COCONUT. Coconut is one of my favorite accent ingredients; it's great in moderation for its adaptability, richness, fragrance, and texture. Coconut milk, extra-virgin coconut oil, unsweetened coconut water, and unsweetened shredded large-flake coconut are all nice to have in your cupboards.

CRUNCHY STUFF. This catch-all category includes things like kale chips (to make your own, see page 234), crumbled brown rice cakes, whole grain croutons, wonton chips (to make your own, see page 104), toasted nuts and seeds, and toasted coconut—for topping soups, adding texture to salads, and boosting grain bowls.

FLOURS. As you move away from all-white flours, there are countless, beautiful whole grain, nut, and seed flours to explore. That said, some of them can be quite pricey. As a result, I tend to limit the flours called for in the baking recipes to a short list of affordable favorites: rye flour, whole wheat pastry flour, and whole wheat flour. I also keep a bag of all-purpose flour on hand to cut some of the heavier, heartier whole grain flours when necessary. Smaller quantities of flours like chickpea/garbanzo and buckwheat are nice to reach for as well.

HINTS OF HEAT. On the feisty, hot front, I lean on harissa, a range of curry pastes, sriracha, cayenne, crushed red pepper flakes, Vietnamese cinnamon, paprika (both hot and smoked), and chile-sesame oil.

MUSHROOMS. Dried mushrooms become the essential foundation for nutrient-packed broths. My preference is for porcini and chanterelles, and you can also make your own dried mushroom blends based on what is available to you locally. Of course, I also love fresh mushrooms for stir-fries, flatbreads, and grilling.

NOODLES. Having a stockpile of noodles means you're just an ingredient or two from a complete meal. Look for soba and brown rice noodles, as well as lentil, whole grain, and chickpea pastas. If your family is on the fence about these so-called healthier noodles, start with a fifty-fifty blend of regular and whole-food noodles—for example, half chickpea penne and half traditional penne—and adjust your percentages from there.

NUT & SEED BUTTERS. Add a bit of creamy richness to dressings, soups, and slathers with nut and seed butters—tahini, almond butter, and peanut butter are all good options. Or make your own nut butters in a food processor and boost them with all sorts of flavors and spices (see pages 252 to 254).

NUTRITIONAL YEAST. Keep these feathery flakes on the counter and use them often. The yeast's savory, nutty, cheeselike flavor adds a serious boost of B vitamins, complete protein, and fiber. Also, I swear it makes my hair and nails grow incredibly fast.

NUTS. Nuts have the ability to deliver both crunch and creaminess. A handful of raw cashews in a blended soup adds silky texture without the need for heavy cream or cheese. Toasted walnuts, almonds, peanuts (technically a legume), and pine nuts are perfect noodle and salad toppers.

OILS. I tend to reach for a good extra-virgin olive oil for cooking, while saving the *great* extra-virgin olive oil for drizzling and the like. Keep little bottles of accent oils like toasted sesame, chile-sesame, walnut, and lemon olive oil in the refrigerator if you're slow to work through them, since these oils can otherwise lose their freshness quickly. Always toss out any oil that smells off or tastes rancid.

PIZZA DOUGH. I make or buy whole grain pizza dough in bulk. If you keep a couple of balls in the refrigerator with some back-up dough in the freezer, pulling together a quick pizza or flatbread meal couldn't be simpler. Bring the dough to room temperature (or thaw) on your counter, add toppings, and bake. I've included a bunch of ideas on page 163.

POWDERS. Potent and pretty, pomegranate, goji, strawberry, raspberry, blueberry, dragon fruit, and green powders made from a range of whole foods that have been dried and crushed make it simple to nutritionally boost smoothies, cereals, batters, and baked goods. Many powders are also effective natural food colorants. If you're curious about taking a dive into the world of adaptogenic powders—natural herbs and substances used to help support and balance the body and increase resistance to stress—see Resources (page 266).

RICE. Although California-grown short-grain brown rice is a go-to for me, there is a beautiful range of whole grain rice available, including brown (and purple) jasmine rice, brown basmati rice, and pink Madagascar or Himalayan rice. Making your own custom blends by combining rice and other small grains (for example, see pages 260 to 263) is another way to increase diversity in your diet.

SALTY THINGS. You'll likely want to keep a few salty options on hand. Salt is one of the punctuations in cooking, helping to bring balance and focus to flavors. Tamari, shoyu, coconut aminos, sea and mineral salts, vegetarian ponzu, and miso can all add a salty flair in their own distinctive ways.

SEAWEED. Nori is great for making wraps, and you can also toast and crush it into a mineral- and nutrient-rich salad or grain-bowl sprinkle. Kombu is a welcome addition to soups and broths, adding flavor, body, and a nutritional boost.

SEEDS. One of the best ways to get healthy fats and oils into your body is by adding seeds to your meals. Keep a range of them on hand, preferably in the refrigerator, because like flavored oils, they can otherwise lose their freshness quickly. My favorites include raw pumpkin seeds (pepitas), sesame seeds, hemp seeds, ground flax seeds, and chia seeds. Always toss out any seeds that smell off or taste rancid.

SOUR ELEMENTS. You often need a little something sour and acidic to balance out a soup, dressing, sauce, or stir-fry. Freshly squeezed citrus juice, apple cider vinegar, white wine vinegar, sourdough bread, yogurt, and kefir are all great options.

SOY. Soy is a beloved component of many traditional, pre-industrial diets, including those in Japan, China, Korea, and Indonesia. Always buy organic and non-GMO versions and try exploring fermented soy ingredients like miso, tempeh, and natto alongside non-fermented ones like edamame, tofu, and soy milk.

SPICES. These are my power ingredients on all fronts. Buy small quantities of spices and (bonus points) freshly grind your own if appropriate—peppercorns, cumin, cardamom, and the like. Store spices in a cool, dark, and dry place. My desert island picks are saffron, caraway, cumin, a shichimi togarashi spice blend, a chana masala spice blend, and a smoked salt.

SWEETENERS. I always stock pure maple syrup, honey, coconut nectar, and a fine granulated sweetener for baking. Organic brown cane sugar (light and dark versions) tends to be the most cost-efficient, but there are an increasing number of options, including coconut palm sugar, date sugar, and jaggery. As far as liquid sweeteners go, keep your eyes peeled for pomegranate syrup and date syrup—both are delicious. And I'm always kicking myself for not using blackstrap molasses more often.

TAMARI. In the soy sauce realm, I generally call for tamari in this book. It's affordable, easy to find, and works when you're cooking for people who need to avoid gluten or wheat (be sure to check the labels). That said, you can substitute soy sauce, shoyu, or coconut aminos in any of these recipes. There is a broad range of concentration, saltiness, and sweetness among these products, so taste as you go and adjust to your liking.

TEMPEH. Tempeh is a beloved Indonesian cultured and fermented soybean cake of sorts. It's worth calling out because when it is good, it is *great*. Tempeh has a stellar nutritional profile and chameleon-like adaptability, and it freezes like a champ. I've included a couple of recipes that feature it (pages 151 and 159), because it is delicious and I always feel great after eating it.

TOMATOES. Keep canned crushed tomatoes and canned whole tomatoes on hand for making lightning-fast sauces and soups. I buy fire-roasted canned tomatoes on occasion, too, when I'm looking for a deeper, less-bright flavor profile. They're great in the Peanut Stew with Spinach & Miso (page 100).

WHOLE GRAINS. Keep jars of your favorite whole grains and cook them when you have a spare moment—whole grain rice, quinoa, and farro are my favorites. Once they're tender, let them cool, and freeze in meal-size portions for easy use later on. You just have to thaw and reheat.

WILD CARDS. This is the fun stuff. I keep dried, edible flowers along with a range of rose and orange blossom waters and extracts. They bring the pretty to baked goods, salads, and the like. Buy makrut lime leaves and curry leaves whenever you come across them. They can both be evasive but worth tracking down because their flavor profiles are wonderfully distinctive. Just double-bag the leaves and pop 'em in the freezer.

"MERCHANDISE" WHAT YOU HAVE

I do one simple task every week that impacts how I feel about cooking more than just about anything else. You might see it as cleaning out the refrigerator, but I think of it as "merchandising" my ingredients. I perform this act in the spirit of a shopkeeper arranging a window display or a fisherman storing row after row of flies in a tackle box.

Each weekend I spend ten minutes or so organizing the fridge. I compost anything that's past its prime. I pull ingredients to the front of the refrigerator if they need to be used ASAP, and I review whatever is hiding in the drawers. If I have a few extra minutes, I like to wash, chop, and otherwise prep some vegetables, then place them in clear jars at the front and center. This allows me to see my cooking palette with a glance and helps me feel bright, excited, and optimistic about our next meal. This little practice also makes a big impact, dramatically reducing food waste. The key is to do this weekly, or, if you have a high-traffic fridge, even more often.

COLLECT YOUR EQUIPMENT

Assembling a kitchen of tools and equipment that fit your cooking style is important. I'm not a fan of having brand-new everything. In fact, I advocate having patience and taking a slow and mindful approach to collecting culinary items—with an eye toward making your cooking a pleasurable and personal experience.

Antique malls, yard sales, flea markets, thrift stores, and consignment shops are all great places to look for affordable kitchen equipment and tableware. Pots, cast iron, vintage dishes, unique cake pans, and linens all tend to turn up in these places, as do single-use appliances you might want to try before splashing out on a more premium version—I'm talking waffle irons, pancake griddles, panini presses, food processors, and the like.

Here's my list of go-tos, but I bet you'll build your own unique all-star collection once you start hunting.

BAKING PANS. Muffin pans, 8- or 9-inch cake pan(s) or glass baking dishes, rimmed baking sheets, and restaurant-style sheet pans.

BLENDER. There are two camps when it comes to blenders. Hand blenders are relatively cheap, convenient to use, and easy to clean, and do a respectable job of pulsing ingredients into creamy soups and dressings. I use mine a lot. That said, if you love to make smoothies, chef-quality silky soups, and next-level dressings, consider investing in a good high-speed blender.

CITRUS REAMER. When you need more than just a squeeze of juice but not enough to justify pulling out the serious juicer.

DIGITAL SCALE. A godsend for quickly and accurately measuring ingredients.

FOOD PROCESSOR. Honestly, I'm on the fence about this one. I reach for my high-speed blender exponentially more often than my food processor. That said, when faced with shredding a mountain of carrots or zucchini, it's a dream to have.

GRATERS. It's nice to have two types: (1) a Microplane-style grater for cheeses, zesting, and fine grating and (2) an old-school box grater for coarsely shredding vegetables, tofu, or fruit.

JARS. Having a collection of all sizes, small to extra-large, is helpful for storing leftovers, grains, rice, and spice blends—and it also helps you phase plastics out of your kitchen.

KNIVES. This topic is a rabbit hole worth diving down and is one of the realms in which you want to invest real time and intention. You're after knives that feel great in the hand, with profiles that are appropriate for your most common tasks. Your knives should age with you as a cook. Generally speaking, instead of investing in a generic knife set, I encourage you to buy one knife at a time. My most-used knives are a beautiful Japanese hand-forged carbon chef's knife, a small Spanish carbon paring knife, and a stainless-steel serrated bread knife. Treat your knives well and they should last a lifetime.

MEASURING CUPS & SPOONS. I like to buy stainless-steel sets of cups and spoons. Glass liquid measuring vessels in 2-cup and 4-cup quantities also get a lot of use.

MIXING BOWLS. A medium-large stainless-steel bowl and large ceramic mixing bowl are both good places to start.

MORTAR & PESTLE. This is a must-have for grinding spices and smashing nuts and seeds, for making dressings and aioli, and for pounding herbs and aromatics into flavor-packed curry pastes. Large and heavy is what you're after here, preferably marble.

PARCHMENT PAPER. This all-purpose kitchen paper is ideal for lining baking pans and sheets and for wrapping treats for friends.

POTS & PANS. Here's another case when I advocate buying one item at a time. Everyone needs to have a big pot for soups, stews, broths, and pasta water. Enameled cast iron is my preferred material because it allows you to go from stovetop to oven, and the larger the pot, the better. A stainless-steel stockpot also does the job, but cooking in cast iron is a dream, so I tend to reach for that one more often. Every cook should have a large cast-iron skillet for everyday use and a medium-size pan for making sauces and reheating soups. Mine is copper, but I used a stainless-steel version for years before that. I keep one PFOA-free (short for perfluorooctanoic acid) nonstick pan on hand to cook scrambled eggs, to make bánh xèo (savory Vietnamese rice-flour crepes), and do omelets.

SPATULA. Strong and semi-stiff for scraping bowls and blenders.

STRAINERS. I use three strainers constantly: (1) a large stainless-steel version for washing greens and straining pasta; (2) a smaller handheld one to rinse rice; and (3) a copper spider strainer about the size of my palm that allows me to easily fish things like broccoli, penne, ramen, or dumplings out of boiling liquids without losing the boil.

WOODEN SPOONS & A ROLLING PIN. I love wood kitchen tools in general because they tell the story of every meal in a way that plastic or silicone can't. Kept dry and treated with a little love (and beeswax with coconut oil), they're the sorts of things you can pass down through generations of family cooks. Every kitchen needs wooden spoons and a rolling pin.

USE YOUR FREEZER

An organized freezer can be your best culinary friend. Frozen homemade curry pastes (see pages 255 to 257) made in big batches are your perfect weeknight flavor bombs. They allow you to put together exciting soups, stir-fries, and broths on a whim. Transfer frozen whole grain pizza dough from the freezer to the fridge in the morning and you'll be ready to turn out your own pizza and flatbread creations (see page 162) by nightfall. The same goes for cooked rice, lentils, and beans. Drained and cooled, these all freeze nicely and can become the foundation of an endless assortment of dishes. I grew up in a household where the freezer was filled with a range of broth and stocks, and I support keeping that tradition alive. Making extra broth or stock (see pages 241 to 243) to keep in the freezer is a surefire way to be nice to your future self.

The freezer is also a great place to store those hard-to-source ingredients like makrut lime leaves and curry leaves. Double-bagged, they'll keep their fragrance and flavor for months. I don't know many curries that wouldn't welcome a showering of either of these leaves, slivered whisper-thin.

Other pantry ingredients worth freezing: cooked hominy for making pozole, seasonal fruit, cookie dough, most soups and stews, and tomato sauce. Just be sure to label *everything* as you freeze it and date it, too.

In an effort to reduce the use of plastics, I deploy a few strategies for freezing foods. For berries, cubed fruit, and cut-vegetable segments (and florets), start by freezing on a parchment-lined baking sheet, then transfer to a freezer-proof glass container once frozen and cover tightly. This reduces clumping and makes it easy to break off as much or as little as you need.

You can also freeze cooked grains, beans, and soups in jars if you're careful and mindful. Use freezer-safe jars with wide mouths and straight sides. Avoid freezing hot foods and allow plenty of headspace in the jar—a couple of inches to be safe—because liquids expand when frozen. Freeze without the lids, then seal the jars tightly once frozen. And don't forget about ice cube trays; they're ideal for freezing curry pastes and other concentrated flavor bombs like pesto and salad dressings. Once frozen, transfer the cubes to a freezer-safe glass container and label.

YOUR OWN PATH

No one loves shopping at a hippie grocery store or co-op more than I do, but this wasn't always the case. The way I eat now is dramatically different from twenty-five years ago. That's when I stopped eating meat (for all the aforementioned reasons). I eventually cleared out many processed ingredients—fake meats and the like—and focused on whole foods and vegetarian meals centered around my farmers' market finds. Now, I cook more whole-food vegan and plant-based dishes inspired by where I'm living or places I've traveled. I'm sure the way I cook and eat will continue to change in the coming years.

That's a long way of saying we're all on our own food path, at our own pace, with our own issues. I've evolved from a very conventional, standard American diet to one that embraces and celebrates beautiful fruits and vegetables along with high-impact ingredients like tempeh, tofu, rye, and soba from traditional cultures. I feel infinitely better eating this way, and I love exploring and experimenting.

If you're reading this book, you're likely searching for ways to use more natural foods or incorporate more vegetarian or vegan meals into your routine. I've tried to include a spectrum of recipes here, and my hope is that you'll find some go-to dishes that meet you where you are so you can continue your journey from there.

At its core, this is a cookbook by a home cook written for home cooks. Remember, every meal cooked for (and with) family and friends is an expression of love and appreciation. It's the food that fuels and nourishes us in the hours and days ahead, impacting strength, mood, and well-being more than just about anything else.

1/ Make-Ahead Mornings

Instant Sriracha Oats

This is a feisty, savory way to start the day. You can use individual packets of unsweetened instant oatmeal or seek out instant oats in the bulk bins of just about any natural foods market. Double or triple the quantities if you're cooking for more than one.

⅔ cup water

⅓ cup unsweetened instant oatmeal

¼ teaspoon tamari, soy sauce, or coconut aminos

1 teaspoon sriracha, or to taste

Sprinkling of toasted peanuts

¼ teaspoon chia seeds

1 tablespoon thinly sliced green onions, white and tender green parts

In a small pot, bring the water to a boil over medium-high heat. Place the oatmeal in a small bowl, pour the boiling water over the top, and stir well. Drizzle the tamari over the oats, dot with sriracha, and top with the peanuts, chia seeds, and green onions. Serve immediately.

SERVES 1

Dirty Chai Baked Oatmeal

A "dirty chai" is produced when a shot of espresso intersects with a masala chai, the much-loved, belly-warming Indian spice-kissed black tea. In this brunch all-star, dirty chai meets baked oatmeal that plumps with coffee aromas and notes of cinnamon and cardamom. The oatmeal can be prepped the night before and baked in the morning if you like.

2 cups old-fashioned rolled oats

1 teaspoon aluminum-free baking powder

Scant ½ teaspoon fine-grain sea salt

1½ cups strongly brewed masala chai in dairy, almond, or oat milk

½ cup strongly brewed black coffee, cooled

⅓ cup pure maple syrup or dark brown cane sugar

1 egg

3 tablespoons unsalted butter, melted

2 ripe bananas, cut into ½-inch slices

Preheat the oven to 375°F and place a rack in the top third. Generously butter the inside of an 8-inch baking dish, or equivalent.

In a bowl, combine the oats, baking powder, and salt. In a second bowl, whisk together the chai, coffee, maple syrup, egg, and 1½ tablespoons of the butter.

Arrange the bananas in a single layer on the bottom of the prepared baking dish and top with an even layer of the oats. Slowly drizzle the chai mixture over the oats. Give the baking dish a few gentle thwacks on the countertop to move the chai through the oats. (At this point, you can cover the dish with plastic wrap and refrigerate overnight or proceed with baking.)

Bake the oatmeal for 35 to 45 minutes, until the top is nicely golden and the oat mixture has set. Remove the dish from the oven and let it cool for a few minutes.

Drizzle the top with the remaining 1½ tablespoons butter and serve warm. Leftovers can be refrigerated and reheated.

MAKES 6 GENEROUS SERVINGS OR 12 SMALL SERVINGS AS PART OF A BRUNCH SPREAD

Granola for Everyone

My California Masala Cluster Granola (page 36) is our house blend, and I make it whenever we have overnight guests. That said, I always make a batch of this version for the kids in my life who like a straightforward cluster granola with the vanilla dialed up—no nuts, no seeds, no spices, no coconut. Use any puffed whole grain cereal.

Preheat the oven to 275°F and place a rack in the center.

Combine the oats and cereal on a rimmed baking sheet. Drizzle the oil across the mixture, followed by the maple syrup and vanilla. Use your hands to mix, until everything is thoroughly coated. Drizzle the egg white over the mixture, sprinkle with the salt, and toss again. Press into an even layer.

Bake for 30 minutes, then rotate the pan halfway, and bake for 10 minutes more, or until the granola is deeply golden.

Remove the pan from the oven and allow the granola to cool completely without stirring. Use a metal spatula to lift slabs of the granola from the pan and break up enough to store in an airtight container for up to 2 weeks.

MAKES 5 CUPS

2 cups old-fashioned rolled oats

2 cups puffed whole grain cereal (millet, kamut, or crisped brown rice)

⅓ cup extra-virgin olive oil

¼ cup pure maple syrup

2 teaspoons vanilla extract

1 large egg white, beaten

¼ teaspoon fine-grain sea salt

California Masala Cluster Granola

Fine-tuned over dozens of batches, this is our house granola. It was inspired by California pantry staples, combined with ingredients gathered on travels to India; it's *extra* clumpy, rose-scented, assertively spiced, and not at all shy. Let this granola get dangerously toasty and golden in the oven, even if you need to cook it for a few more minutes. Also, I call for puffed whole grain cereal or anything along those lines. Serve over yogurt or with a splash of your milk of choice, bake into cookies, or use it to top a fruit salad or add some crunch to your oatmeal.

2 cups old-fashioned rolled oats

1 cup raw cashews

1 cup unsweetened shredded large-flake coconut

2 cups puffed whole grain cereal (millet, kamut, or crisped brown rice)

1½ tablespoons chana masala spice blend (see Note below)

½ cup extra-virgin olive oil

⅓ cup pure maple syrup

1½ teaspoons rose water

1 large egg white, beaten

¼ cup dried rose petals (optional)

Preheat the oven to 275°F and place a rack in the center.

Combine the oats, cashews, coconut, cereal, and chana masala on a rimmed baking sheet.

Drizzle the olive oil across the mixture, followed by the maple syrup and rose water. Use your hands to gently mix until everything is thoroughly coated. Drizzle the egg white over the mixture and toss again. Press into an even layer.

Bake for 30 minutes, rotate the pan halfway, and bake for 15 to 20 minutes more, or until the granola is deeply golden.

Remove the pan from the oven, sprinkle with the rose petals, and allow the granola to cool completely without stirring. Use a metal spatula to lift slabs of the granola from the pan and break up enough to store in an airtight container for up to 2 weeks.

Note: Chana masala spice blends (my favorite is MDH Chana Masala Powder) often include salt, so I omit it in this recipe. If you use a salt-free blend, add a scant ½ teaspoon of fine-grain sea salt with the dry ingredients.

MAKES 7 CUPS

Oat Cereal for Days

This crunchy, low-sugar breakfast cereal is an alternative to store-bought cereals and perfect for busy mornings. Look for an unsweetened O's cereal to use as your base—Trader Joe's has a good version, as do many natural foods markets.

Combine the oat cereal, walnuts, rolled oats, whole grain cereal, oat bran, freeze-dried fruit, and flax seeds in your largest bowl and toss well. Transfer the mixture to two XXL containers (Weck 2.5-liter glass jars are perfect) or a few gallon-size plastic bags. Stored at room temperature, the cereal will keep for 2 to 3 weeks.

Serve with milk or yogurt and lots of toppings.

MAKES ABOUT 10 CUPS

1 (15-ounce) box oat O's cereal

1 cup toasted walnuts, chopped

2 cups quick-cooking rolled oats

3 cups puffed whole grain cereal (millet, kamut, or crisped brown rice)

1 cup oat bran

2 cups freeze-dried fruit (strawberries or raspberries)

⅓ cup ground flax seeds

Milk of choice or plain Greek yogurt, to serve

Fresh berries, sliced banana, chia seeds, or hemp seeds, to top

Multigrain Waffles & Pancakes with Variations

Add a carton of buttermilk and a few eggs to this mix and you're in business. I love these waffles or pancakes for weekdays, camping, and cabin weekends. Be sure to check out the variations to up your breakfast game.

Waffle & Pancake Mix

½ cup old-fashioned rolled oats

1 cup whole wheat or rye flour

2 cups all-purpose flour

Scant 1 cup organic cornstarch or rice flour

2 teaspoons fine-grain sea salt

2 teaspoons aluminum-free baking powder

1 teaspoon baking soda

4 cups buttermilk

4 eggs

2 tablespoons extra-virgin olive oil, plus more to cook

To prepare the mix, combine the oats, whole wheat and all-purpose flours, cornstarch, salt, baking powder, and baking soda in a large airtight container and mix well. Stored at room temperature, the mix will keep for a month or so.

To make waffles or pancakes, whisk together the buttermilk, eggs, and oil in a large bowl. Add the waffle and pancake mix and carefully fold together into a uniform batter (don't overmix).

Oil a waffle iron or skillet. Use a scoop to ladle the batter into your heated cooking vessel and cook until golden and crisp. Transfer the waffles or pancakes to a 225°F oven while you make the rest. Store any leftover batter in an airtight container in the refrigerator for up to 2 days.

MAKES 16 BELGIAN-STYLE WAFFLES OR 24 (4-INCH) PANCAKES

Variations

BIG GREEN WAFFLES: Add 1 cup minced spinach and 1 tablespoon green vegetable powder, such as kale, spinach, spirulina, or wheat grass (optional), to the batter. You can also add up to ⅓ cup crumbled feta cheese and ¼ cup sliced kalamata olives.

WHEAT GERM WAFFLES: Substitute wheat germ for the rolled oats.

LEMON-TURMERIC WAFFLES: Add ½ teaspoon ground turmeric, zest of 1 lemon, and 1 tablespoon poppy seeds to the batter.

RYE WAFFLES: Substitute rye flour for the whole wheat flour.

SAVORY CONFETTI WAFFLES: Add 1 cup grated carrots and ½ cup chopped green onions or chives to the batter.

BANANA-BLUEBERRY (OR RASPBERRY) WAFFLES: Add a well-mashed banana and 1 cup blueberries or raspberries to the batter.

Avocado–Kale Chip Toast

Living in Los Angeles, I've seen avocado toast done a hundred different ways. This is how I like to make it at home. Oat bread is my preference here, but any good whole grain bread will do. And note that your avocado must be at peak ripeness. My favorite way to bake kale chips is on page 234 but feel free to use store-bought if you're short on time. And if you keep Oven-Roasted Cherry Tomatoes (page 236) on hand, by all means, add a few of those as well.

Toast the bread and rub it front and back with the garlic clove. I add the tiniest drizzle of oil to my toast as a primer, but you can certainly skip it. Mash the avocado onto one side of your toast and dust it lightly with salt. Sprinkle with the yeast and kale chips. Finish with the olives and serve immediately.

SERVES 1

A thick slice of multigrain bread

1 clove garlic

1 teaspoon extra-virgin olive oil (optional)

¼ ripe avocado

Fine-grain sea salt

1 tablespoon nutritional yeast

2 tablespoons Crispy Curly Kale Chips (page 234) or store-bought kale chips

3 oil-cured olives, pitted and chopped (optional)

Deviled Egg Toast

This toast requires top-quality bread and a heavy hand with extra toppings; they make all the difference. You can prepare the deviled egg spread up to 3 days ahead of time. It's also a crowd pleaser served on multigrain waffles (see page 40), on Nutritional Yeast Biscuits (page 205), or alongside Lemon-Garlic Pita Chips (page 60).

1 dozen eggs

¼ cup plain Greek yogurt

1 tablespoon extra-virgin olive oil

Scant ½ teaspoon fine-grain sea salt

2 teaspoons Dijon-style mustard

3 tablespoons minced white onion

4 to 6 slices whole grain bread

Paprika, chopped chives, toasted sesame seeds, and/or crushed Crispy Curly Kale Chips (page 234), to top

Place the eggs in a large pot and fill it with cold water to cover the eggs by ½ inch. Bring the water to a gentle boil over medium-high heat, then turn off the heat and cover the pot. Let the eggs sit for exactly 10 minutes.

In the meantime, prepare a large bowl of ice water. When the eggs are done cooking, use a slotted spoon to transfer them to the ice bath to cool. Peel the eggs.

To make the deviled egg spread, cut each egg in half and use a spoon to scoop the yolks into a bowl. Reserve the empty whites for another use. (I like to chop them for fried rice.) Mash and fluff the yolks with a fork, then add the yogurt, 1 teaspoon of the olive oil, the salt, mustard, and onion. Continue to mix and mash until the yolk mixture is creamy and cohesive.

Toast or grill the bread and slather each slice generously with the egg spread. Sprinkle the toasts with paprika, drizzle with the remaining 2 teaspoons olive oil, and finish with any or all of the toppings. Serve immediately.

SERVES 4 TO 6

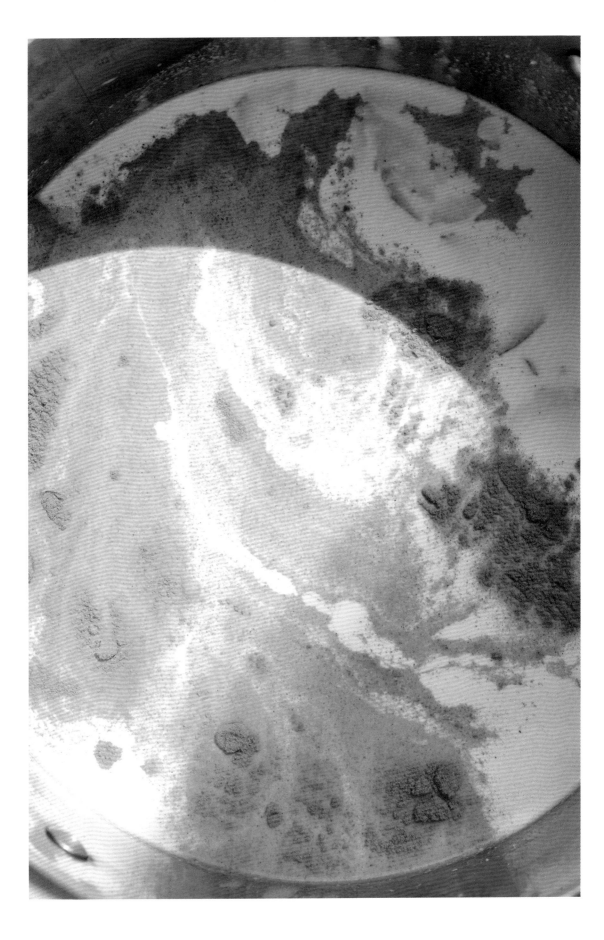

Turmeric-Coconut Ricotta

Garlic and ginger-bolstered, this fragrant, creamy ricotta will spoil you for any store-bought ricotta. Spread it on toast or enjoy it on its own. Here are a couple of tips: avoid ultra-pasteurized milk; pasteurized is fine. Use the slightly tangy, leftover whey liquid in place of broth in soups, curries, and noodle bowls. It's so incredibly tasty and a shame to waste.

Combine the milk, coconut milk, ginger, turmeric, sea salt, and garlic in a large pot over medium-low heat. Slowly bring to a simmer, stirring regularly. When the milk begins to simmer, stir in the lemon juice and continue to heat. The milk should begin to curdle; if it doesn't, add more lemon juice, a splash at a time.

Drain the ricotta mixture through a fine-mesh strainer or cheesecloth into a clean bowl, pressing out as much moisture (whey) as possible; reserve the whey for another use. The ricotta will continue to thicken and drain as it cools.

Serve the fresh cheese topped with a drizzle of oil and a sprinkling of sesame seeds. Store any leftover cheese in an airtight container in the refrigerator for up to 4 days.

MAKES 2 CUPS

½ gallon full-fat whole milk

14-ounce can full-fat coconut milk

4 (¼-inch-thick) slices fresh ginger, peeled and smashed

1 teaspoon ground turmeric

1 teaspoon fine-grain sea salt

4 cloves garlic, smashed

⅔ cup freshly squeezed lemon juice (from about 4 lemons), plus more as needed

Extra-virgin olive oil and sesame seeds, to serve

French Onion Breakfast Strata

This is where French onion dip meets savory bread pudding; it's the perfect make-ahead brunch headliner. Pull everything together the night before you want to serve the strata and bake it the following morning. Look for an organic, all-natural French onion dip blend in the spice aisle of your grocery store or use my French Onion Salt.

2 tablespoons extra-virgin olive oil, plus more to grease and drizzle

1-ounce packet French onion dip mix or ½ cup French Onion Salt (page 235)

2 cups dairy, almond, or oat milk

6 eggs, beaten well

4 cups day-old ½-inch whole grain bread cubes

⅓ cup grated Gruyère cheese

1 bunch chives, minced

Rub a small splash of olive oil across an 8-inch baking dish, or equivalent.

In a medium bowl, whisk together the oil, onion dip mix, and milk. Add the eggs and whisk well again. Arrange the bread cubes in the prepared baking dish in an even layer. Very slowly, drizzle the liquid mixture over the bread and sprinkle with the cheese. Cover the dish and refrigerate overnight.

When you are ready to bake, preheat the oven to 350°F and place a rack in the center.

Bake the strata, uncovered, for 45 to 55 minutes, until the egg is set and puffy and the edges are golden brown. (Cut into it to be sure it is well cooked.)

Serve the strata warm, drizzled with a bit of olive oil and sprinkled with chives.

SERVES 6 TO 8

Jasmine-Chia Breakfast Pudding

I use fragrant jasmine green tea as a portion of the liquid in this breakfast pudding. Its floral flavor is pretty to your taste buds and unexpected. You can, of course, experiment with different teas here; each one brings its own personality. Saffron tea is another favorite, as is strong lemon chamomile tea or tulsi cinnamon tea. Basically, if you have a favorite, try it here! The toppings make or break this dish, so don't skimp.

In a medium bowl, combine the tea, milk, and chia seeds. Add the maple syrup to taste and blitz with a hand blender about ten times, until combined. Place the bowl in the refrigerator until the pudding is thick and scoopable, 30 minutes or overnight.

Serve with any or all of the toppings.

SERVES 4

1½ cups cold jasmine green tea

1½ cups dairy, almond, or oat milk

½ cup plus 1 tablespoon chia seeds

Pure maple syrup, honey, or coconut nectar

Smashed berries, quinoa crispies or crisped brown rice cereal, crushed dried rose petals, and/or toasted almonds, to top

2/
Snacks & Other Quick Bites

Lemon-Pepper Root Chips

When you're ready to move on from standard potato chips, this is the way to go. Colorful store-bought root chips, made from sweet potato, yucca, beets, or purple spuds, bring vibrant hues, crunch, and diverse flavors to your snack spread. I like them served hot, straight from the oven, showered with onions and chives, then kissed with flecks of lemon zest.

5 ounces root vegetable chips

1½ tablespoons extra-virgin olive oil

2 green onions, white and tender green parts, chopped

¼ cup chives, minced

Zest of 1 lemon

½ teaspoon freshly ground black pepper

Preheat the oven to 400°F and place a rack in the center.

Spread the chips evenly on a baking sheet and bake for about 5 minutes, until the chips are golden and toasted.

Remove the baking sheet from the oven. Drizzle the chips with the oil and use tongs to gently toss. Sprinkle with the green onions, chives, lemon zest, and pepper and gently but thoroughly toss again. Transfer the chips to a serving bowl and serve hot.

SERVES 6

Green Sesame Chips

I like to use structured, tortilla-like chips made from leafy greens for this snack, and luckily, they're increasingly available in a range of grocery stores. To make a feisty, spicy version, use sesame-chile oil in place of the toasted sesame oil. And be sure to use the white *and* green parts of the green onions.

Preheat the oven to 400°F and place a rack in the center.

Spread the chips evenly on a baking sheet and bake for 3 to 5 minutes, until toasted.

Remove the baking sheet from the oven, drizzle the chips with the sesame and olive oils, and use tongs to gently toss. Sprinkle with the sesame seeds, green onions, cilantro, and avocado and gently but thoroughly toss again. Transfer the chips to a serving bowl and serve hot.

SERVES 6

5 ounces leafy green tortilla-style chips

1 teaspoon toasted sesame oil or sesame-chile oil

1 tablespoon extra-virgin olive oil

2 tablespoons toasted sesame seeds

2 green onions, white and tender green parts, chopped

¼ cup chopped cilantro leaves

1 ripe avocado, cubed

Lemon-Garlic Pita Chips

Crispy, crunchy, and just the right amount of garlicky, these are my go-to chips for serving alongside Creamy Mung Hummus (page 65) and my Pinkest Party Dip (page 66). I cut the chips into wedges in the recipe, but rectangular strips are also great for dipping.

4 pieces whole wheat pita bread

2 tablespoons extra-virgin olive oil

3 cloves garlic, chopped

Zest of 1 lemon

⅛ teaspoon freshly ground black pepper

Fine-grain sea salt

Preheat the oven to 400°F and place a rack in the center.

Cut each piece of pita bread into eight slices (like a pie) and place them in a large bowl. Drizzle the pita with the oil and toss, squeezing gently to work the oil into the bread a bit. Sprinkle with the garlic and lemon zest and toss again.

Place the chips on a baking sheet in a single layer and bake for 5 to 10 minutes, flipping the chips once, until very golden brown.

Remove the baking sheet from the oven and sprinkle the chips with the pepper and salt to taste. The chips will crisp as they cool on the baking sheet. Serve alongside your favorite dips and spreads. The chips taste best the day they're baked, but you can store leftovers in an airtight container on the counter for up to 1 week.

SERVES 4 TO 6

Puffed Rice Party Mix

This is my version of Chex Mix but arguably more versatile: packed with nuts and seeds, crisped brown rice, nori flakes, and an assertive spice blend that is equal parts chile, brown sugar sweetened, and turmeric-earthy. It is good by the handful at a party but also great sprinkled on salads or over creamy-textured soups. The makrut lime leaves are completely optional but can be a wonderful, fragrant wild card addition if you have them on hand. Keep your eyes peeled in the produce (and freezer) sections of Thai and Cambodian grocery stores and buy a bunch when you see them.

Preheat the oven to 350°F and place racks in the top and bottom third.

In a large bowl, combine the cereal, nuts and seeds, and coconut. Tear or cut the nori into small, bite-size pieces and add them, along with the lime leaves, to the bowl. Drizzle the mixture with the oil and toss well. (Really go for it.)

Divide the mixture between two rimmed baking sheets. Bake for 15 to 20 minutes, stirring once or twice along the way, until the coconut and nuts are deeply golden.

In the meantime, make the spice blend. Combine the cayenne, turmeric, sugar, and salt in a small bowl.

Remove the party mix from the oven, sprinkle immediately with the spice blend, and stir well. Serve immediately or let the mix cool completely and store in an airtight container for up to a month.

MAKES 7 CUPS

3 cups crisped brown rice cereal

¾ cup raw peanuts

¾ cup raw cashews

½ cup raw pumpkin seeds (pepitas)

½ cup unsweetened shredded large-flake coconut

2 (8-inch) sheets nori

7 makrut lime leaves, slivered (optional)

⅓ cup extra-virgin olive oil

Spice Blend

1 teaspoon cayenne pepper

½ teaspoon ground turmeric

2 tablespoons dark brown cane sugar or coconut sugar

½ teaspoon fine-grain sea salt

Smoky Saffron Dates

When you include these in any appetizer spread, they're sure to be the sleeper hit. They're not pretty—but they're incredibly tasty. If you don't have almond extract on hand, swap in vanilla extract. It's different but tastes equally great. Also, I like to use smoked sea salt to counter the sweet tackiness of the dates, but any sea salt will do the job just fine.

Pinch of saffron

½ teaspoon almond extract

1½ tablespoons extra-virgin olive oil

1½ cups whole pitted dates (12 to 20 dates, depending on size)

2 pinches of flaky smoked sea salt

Preheat the oven to 350°F and place a rack in the top third of the oven.

Place the saffron in a tiny bowl and pour the almond extract over the top. Jostle or stir the mixture until the saffron releases its color. Let it sit for a minute or so, then add the oil.

Place the dates in a small ovenproof baking dish. Pour the saffron mixture over the dates and toss to coat. Arrange the dates in a single layer, sprinkle with the salt, and place in the oven. Let cook for about 10 minutes, until the dates are heated through. At this point, switch the oven to broil and brown the dates just until the tops darken a bit; it's not long at all. (Or, if you're not comfortable using your broiler, just leave the dates in the oven a bit longer.) Serve the dates warm in the baking dish.

SERVES 6

Creamy Mung Hummus

This is the smoothest, creamiest hummus I make. Look for mung beans—tiny, bright green powerhouse legumes—in the dried food bins of natural foods markets, Whole Foods, and the like. They have a mighty nutritional profile, are rich in fiber and protein, are celebrated for their ability to be easily digested, and taste a hint sweeter and "greener" than, say, a standard chickpea. If you remember, soak the mung beans overnight prior to cooking. I often serve this hummus with Lemon-Garlic Pita Chips (page 60).

Place the mung beans in a pot and add water to cover by 1 inch. Bring to a boil over medium-high heat and then turn down the heat and simmer for 25 to 30 minutes, until the beans are tender. Drain thoroughly and let cool.

Add the cooked mung beans to a food processor or blender and pulse a few times. Scrape the paste from the corners once or twice, then add the lemon juice, tahini, garlic, and salt. Blend continuously for 1 to 2 minutes, until well combined.

Add the water a splash at a time and blend until the hummus is smooth, light, aerated, and creamy. Taste and adjust to your liking—adding more lemon juice and/or salt as needed.

Serve at room temperature topped with chives, green onions, sesame seeds, and a drizzle of olive oil.

MAKES ABOUT 2 CUPS

2 cups mung beans

2 tablespoons freshly squeezed lemon juice, plus more to taste

½ cup tahini

1 large clove garlic

½ teaspoon fine-grain sea salt, plus more to taste

⅓ cup ice cold water

Chopped chives, thinly sliced green onions (white and green parts), sesame seeds, and extra-virgin olive oil, to serve

Pinkest Party Dip

The color of this festive bean dip is electric, and the flavor has a hint of earthiness from the beets, brightened with the sunshine of citrus and the heat of chiles. I tend to use cannellini beans, but any creamy white bean will do. Dragon fruit (pitaya) powder takes the hot pink color from the beets and turns it nearly neon, but absolutely don't skip the recipe if you can't find it. Also, if you can get your hands on a habanero chile, swap in a quarter of it for the cayenne. The habanero is nice when paired with the fresh citrus juice for a traditional Yucatecan flavor combo.

2 (15-ounce) cans white beans, drained and rinsed

1 tablespoon dragon fruit (pitaya) powder (optional)

1 (2-inch-diameter) raw red beet, peeled

¼ cup freshly squeezed lemon or orange juice, plus more to taste

2 cloves garlic

¼ teaspoon cayenne pepper or ¼ piece habanero chile

½ teaspoon fine-grain sea salt, plus more to taste

2 tablespoons tahini

Dried rose petals, mixed nuts or seeds (walnuts, hemp, sesame), and/or citrus zest, to serve

Place the beans in a blender or food processor and add the dragon fruit powder, beet, citrus juice, garlic, cayenne, salt, and tahini. Blend for 2 to 3 minutes, until smooth, stopping to scrape down the sides of the blender once or twice along the way. Taste and add more citrus juice or salt as needed.

Serve the dip smeared across a serving platter or in a bowl topped with rose petals, whatever nuts or seeds you like, and zest.

MAKES 4 CUPS

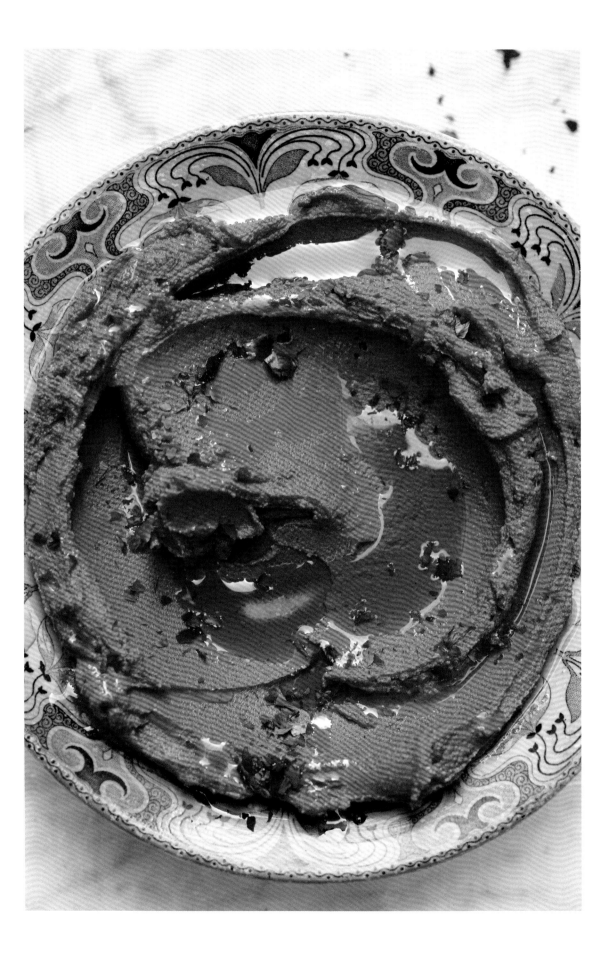

Burrata Ball, Four Ways

I like this as an alternative to a full-blown cheese tray. The burrata is creamy and decadent but doesn't overwhelm your taste buds when flanked by other spreads and delicious bites. If you can't find burrata cheese, a ball of good-quality fresh mozzarella makes a fine substitution.

8-ounce burrata cheese ball

Top the cheese with one of the drizzles below and serve with pita chips, crackers, crudités, and/or grilled flatbread.

SERVES 6

Arugula & Oregano Drizzle

Combine ¼ cup oregano leaves, ¾ cup arugula, 2 cloves garlic, ⅛ teaspoon fine-grain sea salt, and ⅓ cup extra-virgin olive oil in a wide-mouthed jar. Use a hand blender to puree until smooth.

Turmeric-Garlic Drizzle

In a small bowl, smash 1 clove garlic with ¼ teaspoon fine-grain sea salt. Add ¼ cup extra-virgin olive oil and whisk until combined. Sprinkle with ¼ teaspoon ground turmeric and ¼ cup toasted, chopped almonds and stir until smooth.

Spicy Harissa Drizzle

Toast ½ teaspoon caraway seeds in a dry skillet over low heat for 2 to 3 minutes, until fragrant. Transfer the seeds to a mortar and pestle and crush. Add 1 clove garlic and a big pinch of fine-grain sea salt and mash into a paste. Add 1 tablespoon harissa, 3 tablespoons freshly squeezed lemon juice, and ¼ cup extra-virgin olive oil to the mortar and pestle and whisk until smooth.

Stone Fruit & Basil Drizzle

In a bowl, combine ½ cup each of chopped plums, pluots, and peaches. Drizzle the fruit with 3 tablespoons extra-virgin olive oil and sprinkle with 2 or 3 thinly sliced basil leaves.

Golden-Crusted Artichoke Hearts

After noticing frozen artichoke hearts appearing in an increasing number of grocery stores, I couldn't resist adding this recipe. I make these constantly. You cook the frozen artichokes in a skillet, until they're deeply golden on the outside and tender on the inside. These are perfect served on their own but are also right at home with other antipasti or small bites, as a pizza or flatbread topping, and on family-style bowls of pasta. I even add them to big, slurpy noodle soups.

In a large skillet over medium-high heat, add the oil. Stir in the frozen artichokes and cover with a tight-fitting lid. Cook, stirring every few minutes, for 6 to 7 minutes, until the artichokes are tender and golden brown where they touch the pan. At this point, uncover the skillet, add the garlic and salt, and stir well. Cook for another minute. Serve hot or at room temperature.

SERVES 4

2 tablespoons extra-virgin olive oil

1 (12-ounce) bag frozen artichoke hearts

3 cloves garlic, minced

¼ teaspoon fine-grain sea salt

Garlic-Boosted Guacamole

This pumped-up guacamole is for all of you garlic fans out there. It's not only great for dipping into with chips, but also makes a wonderful spread on sandwiches or toast or dolloped on tacos.

2 large ripe avocados, halved

2 teaspoons freshly squeezed lemon juice

3 tablespoons minced white onion

Scant ½ teaspoon fine-grain sea salt

3 tablespoons extra-virgin olive oil

4 cloves garlic, minced

1 serrano chile, seeded and chopped (optional)

2 tablespoons toasted sesame seeds or hemp seeds

Scoop the avocado flesh into a bowl. Add the lemon juice, onion, and salt. Mash the avocados with a fork and spread across your serving bowl.

Place the olive oil, garlic, and chile in a cold small pan or skillet. Turn the heat to medium and sauté for just a minute or so, until warm and fragrant but not long enough to brown the garlic. Spoon the warm garlic and chile mixture over the guacamole with as much (or as little) of the garlic-infused oil as you like. Finish by sprinkling with the seeds. Serve immediately.

MAKES 2 CUPS

3/

The Best Salads

Crunchy Peanut & Saffron Citrus Salad

A colorful citrus salad will brighten any winter day, and the process of blooming saffron in fragrant almond extract to use as a finishing drizzle makes this one exceptional. Use whatever mix of citrus you like here: mandarin, orange, pomelo, grapefruit, tangerine, and/or blood orange are all welcome. To make this more of a meal, serve it over cooked French lentils (lentilles du Puy).

½ teaspoon almond extract

15 threads saffron

3 tablespoons minced red onion

1½ tablespoons freshly squeezed lemon juice

¼ teaspoon fine-grain sea salt, plus more to taste

6 oranges or your favorite citrus (around 3 pounds)

⅓ cup toasted peanuts

1 tablespoon extra-virgin olive oil

Put the almond extract in a small bowl and sprinkle the saffron on top. Swirl the mixture around a bit and then set aside.

Combine the onion, lemon juice, and salt in a second small bowl and set aside as well.

Peel the oranges, slice them crosswise into ½-inch-thick wheels, and slice or tear the wheels into segments (see photo). Arrange the segments in a single layer on a large plate. Sprinkle the citrus with the peanuts.

Add the oil to the onion mixture and stir to combine. Sprinkle the mixture across the citrus and dot the saffron-almond extract all across the top. Taste and add a sprinkling of salt as needed.

SERVES 4

Winter Caprese Salad

The best caprese salads (and sandwiches) are summer fare, gracing tables when tomatoes are sun-ripe and flavorful and basil is bright and fragrant. Later in the year, I do this version with kale, sun-dried tomatoes, basil oil, and good mozzarella. If you remember, puree the basil when it's in season with extra-virgin olive oil, then freeze it, and use it throughout the year. Or seek out a nice basil olive oil. Make this salad a meal by serving it tossed with a favorite pasta or as the finishing touch on a pizza or flatbread (see page 162). You can also make it creamy by adding 2 tablespoons of buttermilk to the dressing.

Chop the kale into bite-size strips and pieces and place in a large salad bowl.

In a wide-mouth jar, sprinkle the garlic with the salt and smash it into a paste. Whisk in the oil and lemon juice. Taste and add more salt or lemon juice as needed.

Pour most of the dressing over the kale and use your hands to really massage it for a minute or two, until the kale softens up. Add the tomatoes and walnuts and toss well. Place the mozzarella pieces on top and drizzle with a bit of oil. Serve immediately.

SERVES 4

2 medium heads lacinato kale (dinosaur kale), stems trimmed and ribs removed

1 clove garlic, minced

¼ teaspoon fine-grain sea salt, plus more to taste

3 tablespoons basil olive oil or extra-virgin olive oil, plus more to serve

1 tablespoon freshly squeezed lemon juice, plus more to taste

¼ cup sun-dried tomatoes packed in oil, drained and chopped

1 cup toasted walnuts

3 ounces mozzarella cheese, torn

Asparagus Salad with Lemony Toasted Pine Nuts

Salads don't get any simpler than this: it's just asparagus, garlic, pine nuts, and lemon. Flecks of the citrusy zest provide a jolt of brightness to each bite. If you have access to Meyer lemons, they'll add a wonderful flavor twist. Use any good-quality thin or medium-thick asparagus here.

1 pound asparagus, ends trimmed

2 cloves garlic

¼ teaspoon fine-grain sea salt

½ cup deeply toasted pine nuts

2 tablespoons extra-virgin olive oil

Zest of 1 lemon

Bring a large pot of salted water to a boil. Add the asparagus and boil for just 30 seconds or so, until the asparagus is bright green. Drain the asparagus and run it under cold water to stop the cooking. Shake off as much water as possible and lay the asparagus on a serving platter.

In a mortar and pestle, smash the garlic together with the salt into a paste. Add the pine nuts and smash until the nuts break down to a chunky texture. Stir in the oil and lemon zest.

Serve the asparagus topped with the lemon–pine nut mixture.

Note: I find it's worth peeling the lemon zest if you're game. Use a peeler instead of a Microplane grater, being mindful to omit any of the white pith. Then hand-chop the peel for a big flavor boost.

SERVES 4

Variations

Use broccoli florets in place of the asparagus.

Use toasted almonds in place of the pine nuts.

Use orange zest in place of the lemon zest.

Five-Minute Bean Salad

Marjoram, with a flavor slightly more floral and less brash than oregano, is one of the most underused herbs. That said, fresh oregano is an equally vibrant plan B. This bean salad is a perfect accompaniment to a meal-size green salad and a platter of summery roasted vegetables. Use 4 cups of your favorite cooked heirloom beans as an alternative to canned beans. When I have extra time and gigante or corona beans on hand, I like to pan-fry them in a bit of olive oil until they're golden-crusted, then proceed with the recipe from there.

Place the beans in a medium serving bowl.

In a blender, combine the marjoram, parsley, garlic, salt, and oil. Pulse until smooth. Toss the dressing with the beans and ¼ cup of the almonds.

Serve the salad topped with the remaining ¼ cup almonds and the lemon zest.

SERVES 6

2 (15-ounce) cans white beans, drained and rinsed

¼ cup marjoram or oregano leaves

¼ cup fresh flat-leaf parsley

3 cloves garlic

¼ teaspoon fine-grain sea salt

⅓ cup extra-virgin olive oil

½ cup toasted sliced almonds

Finely grated lemon zest, to serve

Telegraph Rainbow Salad

When I was in high school, we would drive an hour to Berkeley for concerts, nose rings, vintage shopping on Telegraph Avenue, and *that* salad. It was a colorful, fully loaded leafy salad we all loved, and it would power our day. Crunchy lettuces, mixed beans, seeds, carrot coins, and croutons were all staples, with a creamy, but not-too-creamy, zesty dressing. If you're looking for a meal-size salad, this is it. And, by all means, if you have radicchio, add some of that as well. This is great with the orange-tahini dressing included here, or use any of the dressings on pages 246 to 249.

4 or 5 handfuls of baby romaine or Little Gem lettuce

Handful of cherry tomatoes, halved

¾ cup kidney beans

¾ cup chickpeas

1 celery stalk, thinly sliced

1 carrot, scrubbed and sliced into thin coins

Big handful of whole grain croutons or crumbled Lemon-Garlic Pita Chips (page 60)

¼ cup tahini

⅓ cup freshly squeezed orange juice

2 tablespoons ponzu or 1 tablespoon tamari

1 teaspoon honey

⅓ cup toasted sunflower seeds, to serve

Shred the lettuce, or leave it intact, and place it in a large bowl. Add the tomatoes, beans, chickpeas, celery, carrot, and croutons.

In a small bowl, whisk together the tahini, orange juice, ponzu, and honey.

Toss the salad well with as much or as little of the dressing as you like; any leftover dressing can be stored in an airtight container in the refrigerator for up to 5 days.

Serve the salad family-style, topped with the sunflower seeds.

SERVES 4

Lentil Super Salad

This nutty, hearty, feel-good lentil salad is made with a long list of power ingredients—fiber and protein-dense lentils, digestion-friendly oregano, brain-benefiting walnuts, anti-inflammatory turmeric, avocado, yogurt, garlic—you catch my drift. Use French lentils (lentilles du Puy), black lentils, or even green split peas. Choose lentils (or split pea equivalents) that maintain their structure throughout cooking, because not all do.

In a medium bowl, combine the lentils, walnuts, avocado, oil, and salt. Toss gently but well.

In a separate small bowl, combine the yogurt, turmeric, oregano, garlic, most of the chives, and a big pinch of salt. Stir until well combined.

Serve the lentils on a platter with the yogurt alongside. Finish with creamy dollops of yogurt, a drizzle of oil, the remaining chives, and a light dusting of turmeric.

SERVES 4

3 cups cooked black or green lentils, at room temperature

1 cup toasted walnuts or sunflower seeds

1 ripe avocado, chopped

1 tablespoon extra-virgin olive oil, plus more to serve

¼ teaspoon fine-grain sea salt, plus more to season

1⅓ cups plain Greek yogurt

½ teaspoon ground turmeric, plus more to serve

2 tablespoons fresh oregano, chopped

2 cloves garlic, minced

¼ cup finely chopped chives

Mushroom, Lime & Herb Salad

You don't have to buy fancy or obscure mushrooms for this herb-centric salad; simple brown or white ones are completely delicious in this preparation. Basically, I use a blend of whatever mushrooms look good at the market (king oyster mushrooms are pictured at right). To clean the mushrooms, brush them off with a damp towel.

8 green onions, white and tender green parts, thinly sliced

Juice of 1 lime, plus more to serve

½ serrano chile, seeded and minced

1 tablespoon tamari or soy sauce, plus more to taste

1 tablespoon extra-virgin olive oil

1 pound mixed mushrooms, sliced ¼ inch thick

Generous pinch of fine-grain sea salt

1 cup chopped mixed fresh herbs (cilantro, basil, mint)

⅓ cup toasted peanuts or other nuts

Combine the green onions, lime juice, chile, and tamari in a large bowl and set aside.

Heat the oil in a large skillet over medium-high heat. Add the mushrooms and season with the salt. Cook for 4 minutes, stir, and cook for a few minutes more, until the mushrooms release their liquid and start to brown. When the mushrooms are deeply golden, remove the pan from the heat.

Add the mushrooms to the onion mixture and gently toss. Stir in the herbs and peanuts, taste, and add more tamari as needed.

Spread the salad on a serving platter and finish with a squeeze of lime.

SERVES 2 TO 4

Variations

MUSHROOM SALAD OVER NOODLES:
Lots of things are great with noodles, and this is no exception. You can serve the mushroom salad with hot or cold soba. Just bump up the amount of lime juice and soy sauce so you have enough dressing.

MUSHROOM SALAD WITH TOFU: For more of a one-dish meal, I like to add a bit of crumbled tofu or steamed tempeh to the mushroom skillet.

MUSHROOM SALAD OVER RICE: This is delicious over just about any type of rice you like: a simple bowl of brown jasmine rice, mixed rice and grains, or congee.

Lemony Carrot Salad

I have been making this vibrant shredded salad using a simple box grater for years. Recently, however, I deployed a food processor and turned this into a much quicker 5-minute endeavor, particularly if you keep toasted walnuts on hand. Serve these carrots as a side with spring rolls, on grill nights, or anytime you want to lighten up and brighten a meal. Leftovers keep well for a couple of days in the refrigerator. They're great tossed with chopped kale or salad greens and could easily become a favorite dumpling filling (see page 156).

In a wide-mouth jar, add the lemon juice, salt, brown sugar, and oil and whisk to combine.

In a food processor using the grater attachment, grate the apple and carrots and combine them in a large bowl. Add most of the dressing and the green onions. Taste and add the remaining dressing if you like. Stir in the walnuts just before serving.

SERVES 6 TO 8

⅔ cup freshly squeezed lemon juice (from about 4 lemons)

Scant ½ teaspoon fine-grain sea salt

2 tablespoons dark brown cane sugar

3 tablespoons extra-virgin olive oil

1 apple, quartered

8 to 10 scrubbed carrots

1 cup chopped green onions, white and tender green parts

1½ cups toasted walnuts

Summer Tomato & Celery Salad

Make this salad in late summer when tomatoes are at their peak. You're after the best, most flavorful tomatoes here. Use whatever fresh herbs you like—dill and cilantro are nice, but basil and chives would also work well. If you're worried about the strength and bite of the raw onion, soak the slices in ice water for 10 minutes, then drain well before using. And here's one other tip: use a white wine vinegar that really tastes good, nothing too harsh. A little detail like this makes a difference in a salad where every ingredient counts.

6 celery stalks, thinly sliced

1 small red onion or shallot, thinly sliced

4 ripe tomatoes, cut into bite-size pieces

⅓ cup chopped, mixed fresh herbs (dill, cilantro, basil, chives)

½ cup toasted walnuts

3 tablespoons extra-virgin olive oil, plus more to taste

¼ teaspoon fine-grain sea salt, plus more to taste

1 tablespoon good-quality white wine vinegar, plus more to taste

Combine the celery, onion, tomatoes, herbs, walnuts, oil, and salt in a large bowl. Toss, drizzle the vinegar across everything, then toss again. Taste and adjust with more oil, salt, and vinegar as needed. Serve immediately.

SERVES 4 TO 6

Variations

Skip the olive oil and vinegar and dress this salad with Smoked Paprika & Sumac Dressing (page 247).

Toast 2 (8-inch) sheets of nori along with the walnuts, until crisp. Then crumble the nori over the salad.

For a kiss of richness, top the salad with a few dollops of crème fraîche or sour cream.

Lime-Spiked Pineapple Salad

The sour green notes of lime alongside licorice-scented fennel seeds play off the explosive sweetness of ripe pineapple in this salad (see photo on previous page). It won't be a surprise that the key to this dish is choosing the perfect ripe pineapple. It should have a healthy green crown and nice yellow undertones. The final test? Put your nose close to the pineapple base and give it a sniff; choose the most fragrant one, the one that smells most like pineapple. This salad can be made a day ahead of time and stored, tightly covered, in the refrigerator. Any longer than that and the structure of the pineapple may be compromised.

½ teaspoon whole fennel seeds, crushed

Pinch of fine-grain sea salt

1 tablespoon freshly squeezed lime juice

3 tablespoons dry white wine

½ teaspoon vanilla extract

1 tablespoon extra-virgin olive oil

½ medium pineapple, cut into bite-size chunks

Combine the fennel, salt, lime juice, wine, and vanilla extract in a small bowl and let the mixture sit for 5 minutes to develop the flavors. Whisk in the oil.

Place the pineapple chunks in a medium serving bowl, add the dressing, and gently toss. Let the salad sit for 5 minutes, toss again, and serve.

SERVES 6

Variation

Cut the pineapple into slabs and grill them before cutting into chunks.

4/
Nourishing Soups & Stews

Peanut Stew with Spinach & Miso

This is a substantial, creamy peanut stew with plenty of spice from a good dollop of curry paste. Use your favorite brand of curry, a homemade paste, or even the ubiquitous Thai Kitchen brand. Canned crushed tomatoes are easy to find (and good here!), but this soup gains extra depth of flavor with canned fire-roasted tomatoes. I thought about making the miso optional, because, really, it is. But it's a nice addition, lending extra body, flavor, and dimension.

3 tablespoons extra-virgin olive oil

1 yellow onion, chopped

¾ teaspoon fine-grain sea salt, plus more to taste

1½ cups diced carrots

3 tablespoons red curry paste

½ cup all-natural peanut butter

1 (15-ounce) can crushed tomatoes or crushed fire-roasted tomatoes

4 cups water

8 ounces frozen spinach, chopped

2 tablespoons miso

1 lime, cut into 6 wedges, to serve

Chopped cilantro, cooked brown rice, or toasted peanuts, to serve (optional)

Heat the oil in a large pot over medium heat. Stir in the onion and salt and cook for 5 minutes. Add the carrots and curry paste and cook for another minute, until fragrant. Stir in the peanut butter, tomatoes with their juice, and water and bring to a simmer. Cook for about 10 minutes, until the carrots are tender. Stir in the spinach, bring the stew back to a simmer, then remove the pot from the heat.

Stir in the miso, taste the stew, and add more salt as needed.

Ladle the stew into bowls and serve each with a wedge of lime and any or all of the suggested toppings.

SERVES 6

Paprika-Spiced Mushroom Stew

Hearty and filling, this stew gets its depth from the paprika. I always make this with smoked paprika, but a good sweet paprika is fine, too. Or experiment with blending the two. When it comes to the mushrooms, you have choices. Use a mix or just stick with a single type, like cremini. I chop the mushrooms into pieces between ¼ inch and ½ inch, but go with your personal preference. If you like bigger chunks, have at it. To clean the mushrooms, brush them off with a damp towel.

Heat the oil in a large pot over medium-high heat. Add the mushrooms, onions, and salt and sauté, stirring now and then, until the mushrooms release their liquid and it evaporates, about 10 minutes.

Stir in the paprika and cook for another minute. Add the water and coconut milk, bring to a simmer, and cook for 3 minutes. Stir in the lemon juice, taste, and add more salt as needed.

Scoop the rice into bowls and ladle the soup over the top. A big dollop of yogurt, lots of dill, and cherry tomatoes to serve are all bonuses.

SERVES 6

Variations

Add a few big handfuls of chopped or shredded cabbage to the pot after cooking the mushrooms but before adding the spices and broth.

For less fat but the same amount of creamy, replace the coconut milk with cashew milk. To make fresh cashew milk, combine 1 cup raw cashews with 2 cups water in a high-speed blender and puree until silky smooth.

3 tablespoons extra-virgin olive oil

1 pound mushrooms, chopped

1½ large yellow onions, diced

1¼ teaspoons fine-grain sea salt, plus more to taste

1 tablespoon smoked paprika

3 cups water or Favorite Mushroom Broth (page 242)

1 cup well-mixed, full-fat coconut milk

Juice of 1 lemon

4 cups cooked brown rice, warm

Plain Greek yogurt, chopped fresh dill, and/or Oven-Roasted Cherry Tomatoes (page 236), to serve (optional)

Cauliflower Soup with Wonton Chips

Topped with golden oven-baked wonton chips, this blended cauliflower soup is a nice combination of cream and crunch and is one of my weeknight favorites.

2 tablespoons extra-virgin olive oil, plus more to grease

12 dumpling or wonton wrappers

1 large yellow onion, chopped

1 zucchini, chopped

3 small new potatoes, cut into ½-inch cubes

1 large head cauliflower (about 1½ pounds), cut into florets

1½ teaspoons fine-grain sea salt, plus more to taste

5 cups water

1 lemon

Sesame seeds, toasted sesame oil, lemon olive oil, or chile-sesame oil, to serve (optional)

Preheat the oven to 350°F and place a rack in the center.

Grease a baking sheet with just a bit of oil and arrange the dumpling wrappers in a single layer. Bake for 5 to 7 minutes, until deeply golden, then remove the baking sheet from the oven and transfer the wrappers to a cooling rack to crisp.

Heat the oil in a large pot over medium-high heat. When the oil is hot but not smoking, stir in the onion. Sauté for 2 minutes, then stir in the zucchini, potatoes, cauliflower, and salt and cook for 5 minutes more, until the veggies start getting a bit tender.

Add the water and bring just to a boil. Dial back the heat and simmer for 7 to 10 minutes, until the cauliflower and potatoes are tender throughout.

Remove the pot from the heat and transfer the soup to a high-speed blender (in batches, if necessary). Alternately, use a hand blender directly in the pot. Blend the soup until smooth. Taste and add more salt as needed and a good squeeze of lemon juice.

Ladle the soup into bowls and serve topped with the wonton chips and any of the suggested toppings.

SERVES 6

Variation

For a richer version, replace 1 cup water with 1 cup full-fat coconut milk.

Sriracha-Tomato Soup

Warming and simple to make, this is a pantry soup if ever there was one. The sriracha brings some vivaciousness to the whole affair. Look for organic, all-natural sriracha, or a sriracha that's free of preservatives and unrecognizable ingredients—you want one that contains simply chiles, vinegar, garlic, and so on. Toasted pepitas tend to be my seed of choice for topping, but sliced almonds come in a close second.

Heat the oil in a large pot over medium heat. Add the onions and salt and cook for 5 minutes, until the onions soften but don't brown. Stir in the sriracha, tomatoes, and water. Bring the soup to a boil, turn down the heat, and simmer for 5 to 10 minutes, until the flavors meld.

Stir in the coconut milk and bring the soup back to a simmer. Remove the pot from the heat and transfer the soup to a high-speed blender (in batches, if necessary). Alternately, use a hand blender directly in the pot. Blend the soup until smooth.

Ladle the soup into bowls and serve with a swirl of coconut cream and a sprinkling of nuts or seeds or over a scoop of brown rice. Either way, you can't go wrong with a big squeeze of lemon juice.

SERVES 6

3 tablespoons extra-virgin olive oil

2 yellow onions, halved and thinly sliced

1 teaspoon fine-grain sea salt

3 tablespoons sriracha

1 (28-ounce) can crushed fire-roasted tomatoes

2½ cups water

1 cup full-fat coconut milk, plus coconut cream reserved from the top of the can, to serve

Toasted nuts or seeds, brown rice, or lemon wedges, to serve (optional)

Coconut-Asparagus Soup

Green curry paste combined with asparagus is always a winning combination. This is particularly true in a stir-fry or in a soup like this one. The curry paste often has wonderful aromatics like shallots, lemongrass, and lime leaves that punctuate the bright and savory asparagus. Here, everything is blended together into bowls of the silkiest, creamiest soup imaginable. Counterbalance the creamy with a generous amount of crunchy toppings.

2 tablespoons extra-virgin olive oil

1 small yellow onion, chopped

½ pound new potatoes, diced

2 tablespoons green curry paste

1 (14-ounce) can full-fat coconut milk

1½ teaspoons fine-grain sea salt, plus more to taste

1¼ cups water, plus more as needed

1 pound asparagus, ends trimmed

1 lemon or lime

Chopped chives and crumbled whole grain crackers or croutons, or crispy wonton chips (to make your own, see page 104), to serve (optional)

Heat the oil in a large pot over medium-high heat. Add the onion and sauté until translucent, 2 to 3 minutes.

Add the potatoes to the pot along with the curry paste, coconut milk, salt, and water. Bring to a boil, reduce the heat, and simmer until the potatoes are tender, 8 to 10 minutes.

In the meantime, cut the asparagus into 1-inch pieces. When the potatoes are tender, add the asparagus to the pot. Cook until the asparagus is bright green and cooked through, 2 to 3 minutes depending on thickness.

Remove the pot from the heat and transfer the soup to a high-speed blender (in batches, if necessary). Alternately, use a hand blender directly in the pot. Blend the soup until silky smooth. If the soup is too thick, add more water (preferably hot), a little at a time, to thin it out. Taste and add more salt as needed.

Ladle the soup into bowls and add a squeeze of fresh citrus juice. Top with chives and something crunchy and serve.

SERVES 4 TO 6

Variation

For a coconut-free version, replace the coconut milk and 1¼ cups water with ½ cup raw cashews and 3 cups water.

Harvest Vegetable & Coconut Curry

You can tweak this recipe a thousand different ways, based on what produce is in season or on what looks best at the market or grocery store. When you use broccoli in place of green beans or asparagus in place of zucchini, this becomes less of a late-harvest curry, but it's still all about seasonal vegetables. I can never resist showering each bowl with crushed peanuts and whatever fresh herbs are on hand and serving it alongside a scoop of simple brown rice.

Heat the oil in a large pot over medium heat. Stir in the onion and a generous pinch of salt. Sauté until the onion softens a bit, a couple of minutes. Stir in the zucchini and green beans and cook for 3 minutes more. Stir in the curry paste, followed by the coconut milk and water. Bring the curry to a simmer. Add the chickpeas and tomatoes and cook until heated through, about 5 minutes. Taste and add more salt as needed.

Ladle the soup into bowls and add a generous squeeze of lime to each one. Top with peanuts and herbs and/or serve with rice.

SERVES 4

1 tablespoon extra-virgin coconut or olive oil

1 yellow onion, chopped

Fine-grain sea salt

1 zucchini, cut into ½-inch pieces

1 cup green beans, halved

1 tablespoon yellow or green curry paste

⅔ cup well-mixed, full-fat coconut milk

½ cup water

1 (14-ounce) can chickpeas

1 cup halved cherry tomatoes

1 lime, quartered

Crushed toasted peanuts and fresh mixed herbs, and/or brown rice, to serve (optional)

Jalapeño-Lime Split Pea Soup

A little chunky, equally creamy, and super nutritious, this split pea soup is my definition of feel-good food. I cheat a little by adding a cup of Mexican-style salsa verde. The tanginess and acidity of the tomatillos cut the density of the soup and bring everything into balance.

2 tablespoons extra-virgin olive oil

1 jalapeño pepper, seeded and chopped

1 white onion, chopped

2 cups dried split peas, picked over and rinsed

1 cup Mexican-style salsa verde

6 cups water, plus more as needed

1 teaspoon fine-grain sea salt, plus more to taste

Juice of 1 lime

Hemp seeds, plain Greek yogurt, extra-virgin olive oil, chopped jalapeño pepper, or lime wedge, to serve (optional)

Heat the oil in a large pot over medium-high heat. Add the jalapeño and onion and sauté until the onion softens, about 2 minutes. Add the split peas, salsa verde, and water. Bring the soup to a boil, dial down the heat, and simmer for 20 minutes, until the peas are cooked through. Stir in the salt and remove the pot from the heat.

Transfer half of the soup to a high-speed blender (in batches, if necessary). Alternately, transfer half of the soup to a bowl and use a hand blender directly in the bowl. Puree half of the soup until smooth, then pour the pureed soup back into the pot. If the soup is too thick, add more water, a little at a time, to thin it out, and bring it back to a simmer.

Stir in a couple of big squeezes of lime juice and taste. Add more salt as needed, a little at a time, until the flavor really pops. Serve with any of the suggested toppings.

SERVES 6

Spicy Citrus & Harissa Carrot Soup

I make this weeknight soup more than just about any other. The classic pairing of orange and carrot is always a crowd pleaser, and choosing your favorite spice paste lets you play around with whatever flavor profile you like. No need to peel the carrots here, just give them a good scrub with the rough side of a sponge. If you don't have harissa but keep red curry paste or sriracha on hand, by all means, substitute one of those.

Heat the oil in a large pot over medium-high heat. And the onion and stir until well coated. Sauté until the onion is translucent, 2 to 3 minutes. Add the harissa, then stir in the carrots. Cook for 2 minutes, then stir in the cashews, orange juice, salt, and water. Cover and simmer until the carrots are tender, 10 to 15 minutes.

Remove the pot from the heat and transfer the soup to a high-speed blender (in batches, if necessary). Alternately, use a hand blender directly in the pot. Blend the soup until silky smooth. Taste and add more water (to thin), salt, or harissa as needed. Add a big squeeze of lemon juice.

Ladle the soup into bowls and top with toasted almonds or sesame-chile oil. Add a final touch of microgreens or cilantro and serve with an orange or lemon wedge.

SERVES 6 TO 8

Variation

Spicy Carrot-Coconut Soup: Replace the cashews and 4 cups water with 1 (14-ounce) can coconut milk and 2½ cups water.

2 tablespoons extra-virgin olive oil

1 yellow onion, chopped

2 tablespoons harissa, red curry paste, or sriracha, plus more to taste

2 pounds carrots, scrubbed and cut into ½-inch chunks

1 cup raw cashews

1 cup freshly squeezed orange juice

1½ teaspoons fine-grain sea salt, plus more to taste

4 cups water, plus more as needed

1 lemon

Toasted almonds or sesame-chile oil, microgreens or cilantro, and orange or lemon wedges, to serve (optional)

NOURISHING
SOUPS & STEWS

Ten-Ingredient Masala Chili

This is an Indian-spiced, plant-based version of a hearty, stick-to-your-ribs chili. The tempeh takes on all the flavors of the spices while lending meaty texture. And a hit of adobo sauce contributes depth of flavor and a good amount of spiciness.

3 tablespoons extra-virgin olive oil, plus more to drizzle

1 yellow onion, finely chopped

3 cloves garlic, minced

1¼ teaspoons fine-grain sea salt

1 tablespoon garam masala

1 tablespoon adobo sauce from can of chipotles

1 (28-ounce) can kidney beans, drained and rinsed

1 (28-ounce) can diced fire-roasted tomatoes

1½ cups water

8 ounces tempeh, crumbled

Sliced green onions (white and tender green parts), chopped cilantro, and Salted Garlic Yogurt (page 240), to serve (optional)

Heat the oil in a large pot over medium-high heat. Add the onion, garlic, and salt and sauté until softened, 5 minutes or so.

Stir in the garam masala and adobo sauce. Cook for 1 minute, until fragrant, then stir in the drained beans and the tomatoes along with their juice. Stir in the water and bring to a simmer. Stir in the tempeh and simmer for 15 minutes.

To serve, ladle the chili into bowls and top with green onions, cilantro, a dollop of salted yogurt, and a drizzle of olive oil.

SERVES 6

Winter Green Miso Soup

Rosemary spiked and winter warming, this super simple blend is an herby take on miso soup. It's incredibly fragrant, and I love it ladled over Weeknight Pot Stickers (page 156) or with any of the suggested serving ideas, especially the soba noodles.

4 cups water

6 tablespoons Winter Green Miso Paste (page 257), plus more to taste

¼ teaspoon fine-grain sea salt, plus more to taste

Warm tofu cubes, soba or brown rice noodles, toasted sesame seeds, or a poached egg, to serve (optional)

In a large pot over medium heat, bring the water just to a simmer, then remove from the heat. (To maintain the beneficial properties of miso, you want to avoid boiling it.) Stir the miso paste and salt into the water. Taste, and depending on how salty your miso is, add a bit more salt as needed.

Ladle into bowls and enjoy as a simple broth or add any or all of the suggested serving options.

SERVES 4

Forty-Clove Chickpea Stew

Simple and satisfying with just the right amount of brothy spiciness, this chickpea-studded stew is an example of one-pot magic. Arrange a short list of ingredients in one pot, let it bake for a couple of hours, and you'll be richly rewarded. If you bought the chana masala spice blend for the California Masala Cluster Granola (page 36), use it here in place of the curry powder. It's a wonderful flavor alongside the chickpeas and garlic. If you don't have that blend, it's not a big deal! Any favorite spice blend or curry powder, or even adobo sauce from a can of chipotle peppers, will likely be a fit here.

Preheat the oven to 350°F and place a rack in the bottom third.

Combine the chickpeas, oil, water, garlic heads, onion, and chana masala in a large ovenproof pot or casserole dish with a lid. Set the pot on a rimmed baking sheet and bake for 2 hours, until the beans are tender.

Remove the pot from the oven and season the stew with salt. Getting the seasoning right is key, so taste and add more salt or chana masala as needed.

Ladle the stew into bowls and top with cilantro and a dusting of Parmesan or feta.

SERVES 8

1 pound dried chickpeas, soaked overnight and drained

3 tablespoons extra-virgin olive oil

8 cups water

2 heads garlic, top ⅓ of each lobbed off

1 yellow onion, halved and sliced into thin crescents

1½ tablespoons chana masala spice blend, curry powder, shichimi togarashi, or adobo sauce, plus more to taste

2 teaspoons fine-grain sea salt, plus more to taste

Chopped cilantro and grated Parmesan or crumbled feta, to serve (optional)

5/

Weeknight Noodles

Som Tum Noodles

Sweet, sour, salty, and spicy—this colorful noodle dish uses techniques and flavors of the Thai dish som tum or som tam, or green papaya salad, as a jumping-off point. Turmeric noodles are combined with a rainbow of vegetables and tossed with a puckery sour ("som"), pounded ("tum") salty-sweet dressing.

8 ounces dried brown-rice noodles

1 tablespoon ground turmeric

⅓ cup tamari or soy sauce

⅓ cup dark brown cane sugar

¼ cup freshly squeezed lime juice

2 serrano chiles, stemmed

3 cloves garlic

1 cup halved cherry tomatoes

⅔ cup grated carrots, green papaya, or cucumber

2 cups chopped kale, stems trimmed and ribs removed

⅓ cup toasted peanuts

Mint leaves, fresh Thai basil leaves and flowers, lime wedges, and grilled tofu, to serve (optional)

Bring a large pot of salted water to a boil. Add the dried noodles, stir in the turmeric, and cook the noodles according to the package instructions. Drain, rinse the noodles with cold water, shake off any excess water, and set aside.

In a small saucepan over low heat, combine the tamari and sugar and simmer for a couple of minutes, until the sugar dissolves. Remove the pan from the heat, add the lime juice, chiles, and garlic and use a hand blender to blend until smooth.

When you're ready to serve, combine the tomatoes, carrots, and kale in a large serving bowl. Add a generous splash of dressing and crush and stir everything with a pestle or a wooden spoon. Add the noodles and toss well with more dressing. Add the peanuts, toss again, and serve topped with mint, basil, and tofu, with any remaining dressing alongside.

SERVES 4

Ditalini "Risotto" with Broccoli & Pine Nuts

This is not a true risotto, of course, but it's cooked in a similar spirit. Any small, short pasta will work here. I love ditalini, but whole wheat orzo is a good alternative.

Heat the oil in a large pot over medium-high heat. Add the garlic and onion and cook until soft, about 3 minutes. Add the beer, bring to a simmer, and cook for about 3 minutes, until the liquid reduces a bit. Stir in the lentils and pasta along with 3 cups of the broth and stir well. Stir in the remaining 4 cups broth, a cup at a time, adding more as it is absorbed. This should take 15 to 20 minutes.

When the pasta and lentils are fully cooked and the broth is mostly absorbed, stir in the Parmesan, broccoli, and salt. Taste and add more salt as needed. Serve the risotto with pine nuts sprinkled on top and a drizzle of olive oil.

SERVES 6 TO 8

3 tablespoons extra-virgin olive oil, plus more to serve

3 cloves garlic, minced

1 yellow onion, minced

⅔ cup lager-style beer, white wine, sake, or vegetable broth

⅓ cup French lentils (lentilles du Puy); optional

1 pound dried ditalini pasta

7 cups vegetable broth or water

½ cup grated Parmesan cheese

1 head broccoli, finely chopped

¼ teaspoon fine-grain sea salt, plus more to taste

⅓ cup toasted pine nuts, to serve

Blistered Cherry Tomato Soba

This beautiful soba-based tangle is built around skillet-blistered cherry tomatoes and accented with lemon zest, mint, broccoli, and toasted cashews. It was inspired by a version of the dish shared with me by Naoko Takei Moore, the queen of Japanese clay pots (donabe) in Los Angeles.

8 ounces dried soba noodles

3 tablespoons extra-virgin olive oil

4 cloves garlic, thinly sliced

1 pint cherry tomatoes

3 cups broccoli or broccolini florets

¼ teaspoon fine-grain sea salt, plus more to taste

⅓ cup chopped mint leaves

½ cup well-toasted cashews, chopped

Grated Parmesan cheese, shichimi togarashi or chile flakes, and lemon zest, to serve (optional)

Bring a large pot of salted water to a boil. Add the soba noodles and cook according to the package instructions for al dente noodles.

In the meantime, combine the oil, garlic, and tomatoes in a large pan or skillet over medium heat. Cook for 3 minutes, stirring occasionally, then add the broccoli. Cook, continuing to stir, for 3 to 4 minutes more, until most of the tomatoes burst and the broccoli is bright green. Remove the pan from the heat and add the salt.

When the soba is cooked, drain it well, and add it to the tomato mixture in the skillet. Stir in the mint and cashews. Taste and add more salt as needed.

Serve the soba in individual bowls with Parmesan, shichimi togarashi or chile flakes, and lemon zest on the side.

SERVES 2 TO 4

Ravioli in Toasted Almond Broth

Kissed with a hint of lemon, this brothy pasta bowl leans on blended almonds rather than heavy cream. Keep your eye out for whole wheat ravioli, as it's increasingly available in grocery stores and natural foods markets. If you can't find it, any of your favorite ravioli will do. Also, if you don't have a high-speed blender, strain the broth after blending through a fine-mesh strainer or cheesecloth. You want it to be silky smooth. In the springtime, I often replace the broccolini with bite-size segments of asparagus.

Bring a large pot of salted water to a boil.

In the meantime, place the almonds and broth in a high-speed blender and blend until smooth. Add the lemon juice, salt, and pepper and set aside.

Add the ravioli to the boiling water and cook according to the package instructions. Add the broccolini to the ravioli in the final minute of cooking.

Drain the pasta and broccolini and divide it among four bowls. Pour the broth over the pasta and top with chives, green onions, almonds, a drizzle of olive oil, and a dusting of cheese. Serve immediately.

SERVES 4

1 cup toasted sliced almonds

2½ cups hot vegetable broth or water

2 tablespoons freshly squeezed lemon juice

½ teaspoon fine-grain sea salt

¼ teaspoon freshly ground black pepper

1 pound of your favorite ravioli

1 bunch broccolini or broccoli florets

Minced chives, minced green onions (white and tender green parts), toasted sliced almonds, extra-virgin olive oil, lemon wedges, and grated Parmesan cheese, to serve (optional)

Any Noodles with Lemon-Nori Oil

Light and bright with assertive jolts of lemon zest and cayenne, plus a bit of crunch from sesame seeds, this dish can be made with a whole range of noodles. Some days it's soba or udon, and other days I go for lentil noodles (see photo).

1 (8-inch) sheet nori, toasted (see Note)

1 bunch chives, minced

½ cup extra-virgin olive oil

¼ teaspoon fine-grain sea salt

Zest of 2 lemons

4 teaspoons toasted sesame seeds

¼ teaspoon cayenne pepper

½ teaspoon ground cumin

1 pound dried noodles of your choice (soba, udon, lentil, chickpea)

½ cup grated Parmesan or Pecorino cheese

Crush or cut the toasted nori into the smallest flecks you can manage. In a small bowl, combine the nori and chives, reserving a bit of each for topping at the end. Add the oil, salt, lemon zest, sesame seeds, cayenne, and cumin to the bowl and set aside.

Bring a large pot of salted water to a boil. Add the noodles and cook according to the package instructions. Drain well, reserving 1 cup of the noodle water. Return the noodles to the pot and place it over low heat. Stir in a little of the reserved noodle water, most of the nori oil, and the cheese and stir well. Add more noodle water, a splash at a time, to loosen up the noodles as needed.

Serve immediately topped with the remaining nori pieces, the chives, and the remaining nori oil.

Note: To toast nori, gently wave it over the flame of a gas burner or bake it on a baking sheet in a 350°F oven until crisped. Cool, then crumble.

SERVES 4 TO 6

Variation

In the springtime, top the noodles with cooked favas and grated Pecorino cheese.

Spicy, Creamy, Carroty Peanut Noodles

Beta-carotene–rich carrots sneak their way into these spicy peanut noodles, adding a nutritional bump and a feisty boost of color. Serve the noodles straight or top them with grilled tofu and crushed kale chips to turn this into a main meal.

Bring a large pot of salted water to a boil. Add the noodles and cook according to the package instructions. Drain the noodles and shake off as much water as possible. Transfer to a medium serving bowl.

In the meantime, combine the peanut butter, ponzu, oil, water, and carrot in a high-speed blender. Blend for a minute or two, until silky smooth. Taste and add more oil if you want it spicier.

Pour most of the dressing over the noodles and toss well. Add more dressing if you like, top with the cucumber, and serve immediately, sprinkled with peanuts and green onions.

SERVES 4 TO 6

12 ounces dried brown-rice or soba noodles

⅓ cup all-natural chunky peanut butter

¼ cup ponzu

2 tablespoons sesame-chile oil, plus more to taste

⅔ cup hot water

1 carrot, scrubbed

1 cucumber, seeded and diced

Peanuts and minced green onions (white and tender green parts), to serve

Green Herb–Soba Bowl

Fast to make and easy to clean up, this soba bowl is an ideal solo lunch. Simply double or triple the amounts if you're cooking for more people. If you want to bulk out your bowl with added vegetables, add handfuls of broccoli or cauliflower florets and/or asparagus segments to the boiling water along with the tofu and stir in a little more harissa and miso.

2 ounces dried soba noodles

3 ounces firm organic tofu, cut into ½-inch cubes

2 teaspoons harissa, plus more to taste

1 teaspoon miso, plus more to taste

Handful each of chopped arugula, spinach, and cilantro with stems

A few drops of toasted sesame oil

White sesame seeds, to serve

Bring a large pot of salted water to a boil. Add the noodles and cook according to the package directions until al dente. In the final 30 seconds of cooking, add the tofu just to heat through. Drain and place the noodles and tofu in a serving bowl. Add the harissa and miso and toss. Taste and add more of either one as needed. Stir in the arugula, spinach, and cilantro. Toss again and finish with the oil and sesame seeds.

SERVES 1

Tangerine & Tahini Ponzu Noodles

This is the sort of low-effort lunch I love: a little something green, a little something citrusy, and a little something creamy, brought together over soba noodles. I call for tangerine juice here, but freshly squeezed orange juice can be easier to come by, and is a fine replacement.

Bring a large pot of salted water to a boil. Add the soba noodles and cook according to the package directions. In the last minute of cooking, add the broccoli and cook until bright green and just tender. Drain, rinse with cold water to stop the cooking, shake off any excess water, and transfer to a large bowl.

In the meantime, in a small bowl, whisk together the tahini, tangerine juice, ponzu, and honey. Stir the mixture into the cooked soba noodles along with the carrots. Taste and add a bit of salt as needed.

To serve, scoop the noodles into bowls and top with tangerine zest, chile flakes, and sesame seeds.

SERVES 2 TO 4

8 ounces dried soba noodles

1 head broccoli, cut into florets

¼ cup tahini

⅓ cup freshly squeezed tangerine juice

2 tablespoons ponzu

1 teaspoon honey

1 carrot, scrubbed and sliced into razor-thin coins

Fine-grain sea salt

Tangerine zest, chile flakes, and sesame seeds, to serve

6/
Single Skillets

Spicy Curry-Banzo Bowl

Chop an onion along with a few mushrooms and this curry-bolstered chickpea (garbanzo) bowl comes together in no time. Leftovers are good baked on top of pizza dough into a flatbread (see page 162) or wrapped into a tortilla along with some brown rice, burrito-style. To clean the mushrooms, brush them off with a damp towel.

2 tablespoons extra-virgin olive oil

1 yellow onion, chopped

¼ teaspoon fine-grain sea salt, plus more to taste

8 ounces brown mushrooms, chopped

1½ tablespoons curry paste (red, green, yellow, or your favorite)

2 (15-ounce) cans chickpeas, drained and rinsed

Chopped mixed herbs (cilantro, basil), freshly squeezed lime juice and zest, and/or hemp seeds, to serve (optional)

Heat the oil in a large pan over medium-high heat. Add the onion and salt and sauté until translucent, about 3 minutes. Add the mushrooms and sauté until they release their liquid and start to brown a bit, 5 to 7 minutes. Stir in the curry paste and cook until fragrant, 1 to 2 minutes.

Pour one-third of the chickpeas into a bowl and smash them with a fork (or your hands). Stir the remaining whole chickpeas and the smashed chickpeas into the onion-curry mixture along with a generous splash of water. Taste and add more salt as needed.

Serve in bowls topped with lots of herbs, lime zest and a big squeeze of juice, and a sprinkling of hemp seeds for crunch.

SERVES 4

Variations

Serve in wraps with a yogurt or tahini drizzle and lots of herbs.

Stir in lots of chopped greens.

Enjoy with garlic naan.

Cool a bit and use as a filling for lettuce wraps.

Scoop over rice.

Top with avocado and toasted nuts and seeds.

Harissa Brunch Eggs with Multigrain Toast

With tomatoes, beans, and a bit of spice, this is a simple, one-skillet brunch hero. Serve it with thick slices of garlic-rubbed toast. Also, feel free to switch up the flavor profile. I typically make it with harissa, but you can use sriracha or red curry paste in its place.

Heat the oil in a large skillet over medium-high heat. Stir in the onion and salt and sauté until the onion softens and becomes translucent, 5 to 6 minutes.

Stir in the harissa and then the tomatoes and beans. Bring to a simmer and cook for 5 minutes, dialing back the heat to keep it at a simmer.

Use a spoon to make little pockets for the eggs near the outer edges of the skillet. Gently break the eggs into the pockets and sprinkle with the feta and olives. Cover and cook until the eggs are set, about 5 minutes.

Rub the toast with the garlic. Serve the eggs in the skillet, showered with chives and lemon zest, with the toast on the side.

SERVES 4

3 tablespoons extra-virgin olive oil

1 large yellow onion, chopped

¼ teaspoon fine-grain sea salt

2 tablespoons harissa

1 (28-ounce) can crushed tomatoes

1 (15-ounce) can cannellini beans or chickpeas, drained and rinsed

4 eggs

½ cup crumbled feta cheese

¼ cup sliced black olives

4 to 6 thick slices multigrain bread, toasted

1 clove garlic

Chopped chives and lemon zest, to serve

Everyone's Favorite Fried Rice

This is what I make when our guests include kids, but adults always love it, too. It's prepared simply with a whole grain take here. Be sure to prep everything before you start cooking because the dish comes together fast. I use anything from brown jasmine and short-grain brown rice to basmati rice. On occasion, I even make this with millet, which earns an A-plus.

1½ tablespoons toasted sesame oil

1 large carrot, scrubbed and finely minced

2 cloves garlic, minced

2½ cups cold cooked brown jasmine rice, short-grain brown rice, basmati rice, or millet

1 cup frozen peas

2 eggs, beaten

2 to 3 teaspoons tamari or soy sauce

Chile-sesame oil, to serve (if your kid likes spicy)

Heat 1 tablespoon of the sesame oil in a large skillet or wok over medium heat. Add the carrot and sauté for 5 minutes, until just tender but not mushy. Stir in the garlic. Wait 30 seconds, add the rice, and stir to separate the grains. Cook for 4 minutes, then stir in the peas and cook until the peas are hot, another minute or two.

Shift the rice and vegetables to the sides of the skillet and add the remaining ½ tablespoon sesame oil to the pan. Add the eggs and push them around a bit, until just set. Break up the eggs with a spatula.

Drizzle in the tamari and stir-fry everything together until well combined, about 30 seconds. Serve immediately with a drizzle of chile-sesame oil.

SERVES 2 OR 3

Green Curry Stir-Fry

Leeks are underutilized, but I'm never sorry when I cook with them. Their crisp, oniony sweetness when browned and caramelized in the pan is a tasty dream. The way they play alongside earthy mushrooms and broccoli in a stir-fry like this? So good. I love to use the Cilantro–Green Curry Paste here, but don't get hung up on that. Use whatever favorite curry paste you have on hand—green is my preference, but yellow or red will work, too.

Heat 1 tablespoon of the oil in a large skillet or wok over medium-high heat. Stir in the tofu and salt and sauté for 3 to 4 minutes, until the tofu just starts to get golden on all sides. Once the tofu starts to take on color, add the leeks. Sauté for 7 to 10 minutes, until the leeks become golden and caramelized. Transfer the tofu and leeks to a bowl and set aside.

Add the remaining 1 tablespoon oil to the skillet along with the mushrooms. Sauté, stirring, until the mushrooms release their moisture and start to brown, 5 to 7 minutes. Add the broccoli and toss well. Once the broccoli is bright green and just-cooked (1 to 2 minutes), add the tofu and leeks back to the skillet.

Combine the warm water and curry paste in a small bowl, then add it to the skillet. Toss and stir well.

Let the vegetables cook for another minute or so before scooping them into bowls or over a bed of rice. Top with sprouts or chives and serve immediately.

SERVES 4

2 tablespoons extra-virgin olive oil

8 ounces extra-firm organic tofu, cut into ¼-inch cubes

¼ teaspoon fine-grain sea salt

2 cups chopped leeks, well cleaned

2 cups mushrooms, sliced ¼ inch thick

2 cups broccoli florets

¼ cup warm water

2 tablespoons Cilantro–Green Curry Paste (page 256), or your favorite green, red, or yellow curry paste

Cooked rice or grains (see pages 260 to 263), to serve

Sprouts or chopped chives, to serve

Big Green Fried Rice

Aromatic, packed with flecks of kale, and punctuated with fresh vegetables, every component of this fried rice delivers. Prep all of your ingredients ahead of time, and if you're doubling the recipe to serve more people, cook it in two batches so you aren't crowding the pan.

1½ tablespoons toasted sesame oil

4 green onions, white and tender green parts, chopped

1 cup sliced asparagus or green beans, trimmed and cut into ¼-inch segments

2 cloves garlic, minced

1 tablespoon peeled and grated fresh ginger

2½ cups cold cooked brown rice

2 cups well-chopped kale, trimmed and ribs removed

2 eggs, beaten

2 to 3 teaspoons tamari or soy sauce

Chile-sesame oil and zest of 1 lemon, to serve (optional)

Heat 1 tablespoon of the sesame oil in a large skillet or wok over high heat. Add the green onions and asparagus and cook for 3 to 4 minutes, until the green onions soften.

Stir in the garlic and ginger. Wait 30 seconds, then add the rice and stir to separate the grains. Cook for about 3 minutes, until the rice is hot, then stir in the kale.

Shift the rice and vegetables to the sides of the skillet and add the remaining ½ tablespoon sesame oil to the pan. Add the eggs and push them around until just set. Break up the eggs with a spatula.

Drizzle in the tamari and stir-fry everything together until well combined, about 30 seconds.

To serve, drizzle with chile-sesame oil if you like a bit of heat and sprinkle with lemon zest. Serve immediately.

SERVES 2 OR 3

Feisty Tofu with Broccoli, Chile & Nuts

This simple but spicy stir-fry is loaded with chiles and nuts—choose cashews or peanuts, whatever you love. Be sure to prep all of the ingredients before you start cooking because stir-fries cook quickly. Serve this over brown rice, soba, or brown-rice noodles.

In a wide, shallow dish, stir together 2 tablespoons of the tamari and the water. Toss the tofu with the tamari mixture. Let the tofu marinate for at least 10 minutes, but really, longer is better, even overnight.

In the meantime, combine the remaining 1 tablespoon tamari, the maple syrup, and sesame oil in a small bowl.

Heat the olive oil in a large skillet or wok over medium-high heat. Add the chiles and cook for 20 to 30 seconds, until they're fragrant and darken slightly. Transfer the chiles to a plate, leaving the oil behind.

Add the marinated tofu to the pan and cook for 2 minutes, until golden on all sides. Transfer the tofu to the plate with the chiles.

Add the broccoli, garlic, ginger, and tamari-maple mixture to the skillet. Stir well and cook, covered, for 1 to 2 minutes, until the broccoli brightens. Uncover the pan and stir in the nuts, tofu, and chiles. Cook for another minute or two, long enough for the nuts to toast a bit, and serve immediately.

SERVES 4

3 tablespoons tamari or soy sauce

2 tablespoons water

12 ounces extra-firm organic tofu, cut into ¾-inch cubes

1 tablespoon pure maple syrup

1 teaspoon toasted sesame oil

2 tablespoons extra-virgin olive oil

7 dried red chiles, stemmed and thinly sliced

3 or 4 handfuls of broccoli florets

3 cloves garlic, chopped

1 tablespoon peeled and minced fresh ginger

½ cup raw cashews or peanuts

Tempeh-Ponzu Balls

Golden-crusted and nutritionally packed, these little veggie balls have become such a favorite. Feel free to adapt the recipe to whatever vegetables you have on hand. I call for cabbage and carrot, but zucchini or chopped kale and spinach are great, too. You can also play with the shape. In addition to making balls, I often shape these into kid-friendly onigiri (Japanese rice triangles; see page 180) or press them into small patties. For added crust, roll each ball in crushed puffed rice cereal before pan-frying.

Place the chickpeas and water in a blender and blend until smooth. Alternately, place the chickpeas and water in a bowl and use a hand blender. Transfer the puree to a large bowl.

Using a box grater, grate the tempeh on top of the beans. Add the flour, yeast, garlic, onion, carrot, cabbage, and salt. Use your hands to combine everything. And I mean really get in there and mix it all together. Using a tablespoon, shape the mixture into balls. At this point, you can refrigerate the balls in an airtight container for up to 3 days.

To cook the tempeh, heat the oil in a large skillet over medium-high heat. Add half of the balls and cook for 7 to 9 minutes, shaking the skillet regularly to keep the balls from sticking, until they are deeply golden on all sides. Remove the tempeh from the skillet and cook the remaining balls.

Serve immediately, sprinkled with chives and drizzled with ponzu or serve the ponzu on the side as a dipping sauce.

MAKES 30 BALLS

1 (15-ounce) can chickpeas or white beans, drained and rinsed

1 tablespoon water

8 ounces tempeh

3 tablespoons whole wheat, rye, almond, or buckwheat flour

1 tablespoon nutritional yeast

3 cloves garlic, chopped

¼ cup minced yellow onion

½ cup finely chopped carrot

½ cup finely chopped green cabbage

¼ teaspoon fine-grain sea salt

1 tablespoon extra-virgin olive oil

⅓ cup chopped chives

¼ cup ponzu

Jalapeño-Cheddar Socca

The flow of vegetables from our community garden plot is substantial, and these little pancakes are one way I put a dent in that flow. The chickpea flour base is a simple socca batter—the kind that's popular in some coastal Mediterranean cities like Nice. I use buttermilk for tenderness and tang, but thinned-out yogurt or water will also work. You'll see spinach and carrots in the recipe, but loading up the batter with just about any quick-cooking grated vegetable is fair game. You can make the batter a day or two ahead of time and store it in an airtight container in the refrigerator until you're ready to cook.

1½ cups chickpea (garbanzo bean) flour

2 eggs

1½ cups buttermilk

3 tablespoons extra-virgin olive oil, plus more to grease

¾ teaspoon fine-grain sea salt

2 large carrots, scrubbed

⅔ cup chopped spinach

1 jalapeño pepper, stemmed and chopped

¼ cup grated Cheddar cheese

Salted Garlic Yogurt (page 240), to serve (optional)

Combine the flour, eggs, buttermilk, oil, and salt in a large bowl.

Use a vegetable peeler to shave the carrots into thin ribbons. Use a knife to mince the carrot ribbons into tiny flecks; you should have about ¾ cup.

Add the carrots, spinach, jalapeño, and cheese to the bowl and whisk until the batter is smooth. Allow it to sit for 10 to 15 minutes to allow the flour to hydrate.

Drizzle a small amount of oil into a large skillet or griddle over medium-high heat. When the oil is hot but not smoking, spoon three or four generous dollops of batter into the pan with room between them. Spread each into a pancake shape and cook until golden brown, 3 to 4 minutes per side. Transfer to plates and serve as is or dolloped with yogurt.

MAKES 12 PANCAKES

Variations

BEET & FETA SOCCA: Replace the carrots, spinach, jalapeño, and Cheddar with 1 cup grated beets and ⅓ cup crumbled feta cheese.

SUMMER HARVEST SOCCA: Replace the carrots, spinach, jalapeño, and Cheddar with ¾ cup grated zucchini, ½ cup chopped tomatoes, and ¼ cup grated Gruyère cheese.

BROCCOLI-CHEDDAR SOCCA: Replace the carrots, spinach, and jalapeño with ¾ cup finely chopped broccoli and add an additional ¼ cup grated Cheddar cheese.

Weeknight Pot Stickers

My dad regularly made pot stickers when I was a kid, and my job was to help him fold and crimp. To this day, I love to make quick dumplings from whatever's in the fridge. This version, using leftover Lemony Carrot Salad, is a standout. The residual lemon dressing marinates the tofu, and toasted walnuts bring the crunch. You can cook these from frozen, and if you can't find round wrappers, buy square ones and fold them into triangles on the diagonal. (See photos on pages 154 and 155.)

1½ cups leftover Lemony Carrot Salad (page 91)

1½ cups finely crumbled extra-firm organic tofu

All-purpose flour, for dusting

1 packet round dumpling wrappers

1 tablespoon extra-virgin olive oil

⅓ cup water

Ponzu and sesame-chile oil, to serve

Combine the carrot salad and tofu in a bowl and mix well. Set the filling aside.

Generously sprinkle flour on a plate or baking sheet, then very lightly dust your countertop with flour. Place 12 wrappers on the floured countertop and add a small dollop of filling just off-center of each dumpling. Run a wet finger around the rim of each wrapper and press the edges together well; try to avoid trapping air bubbles. Start at one edge and pleat each dumpling numerous times along the seam (see photo on page 155). Gently press each one down against the counter to give it a flat base. Repeat until you run out of wrappers or filling.

Place the dumplings, seam-side up, on the prepared plate. Any flour that sticks to the dumpling base will give it extra crunch. At this point, you can freeze the dumplings in an airtight container for up to a month.

To cook, heat ½ tablespoon of the oil in a large skillet over medium-high heat. Arrange the dumplings in the pan, seam-side up, with space between each so they don't stick together. Pan-fry, in batches if necessary, until the bottoms are deeply golden, 2 to 3 minutes. With a large lid in one hand, carefully and quickly add the water to the pan, immediately cover, and cook the dumplings for a few minutes, until the water is nearly evaporated. Uncover and finish cooking until all of the water is gone, 1 to 2 minutes more.

Serve the dumplings drizzled with ponzu and sesame-chile oil.

SERVES 4

Buttermilk-Farro Risotto

While this risotto might sound rich and indulgent, adding a big splash of buttermilk once the farro is plump and tender creates a delicious tanginess that lets you scale back a lot on the cheese. And using semi-pearled farro helps to achieve risotto's signature creaminess. If you can't find farro, semi-pearled barley works well, too. Finish with just a bit of Parmesan or Gruyère cheese for a relatively light risotto. To clean the mushrooms, brush them off with a damp towel.

In a large saucepan over medium-high heat, combine the oil, shallots, and garlic. Sauté for about 5 minutes, until the shallots have softened, then stir in the mushrooms. Cook for about 4 minutes, until the mushrooms take on a bit of color. Stir in the farro and salt and cook for 1 minute more.

Add 2 cups of the hot water and simmer for 3 to 4 minutes, until the farro has absorbed some of the liquid. Adjust the heat to maintain an active but gentle simmer. Add the remaining 6 cups hot water in increments of 2 cups, letting the farro absorb most of the liquid before adding more water. This should take between 40 and 45 minutes in total. Stir the risotto regularly so the grains on the bottom of the pan don't scorch.

When the farro is tender, remove the pan from the heat and let it rest for 4 minutes. Stir in the buttermilk and ¼ cup of the cheese.

Scoop the risotto into bowls and serve topped with the remaining cheese and the olives.

SERVES 6

3 tablespoons extra-virgin olive oil

3 shallots, chopped

4 cloves garlic, chopped

½ pound brown mushrooms, finely chopped

1 pound semi-pearled farro or semi-pearled barley

¾ teaspoon fine-grain sea salt

8 cups hot water

½ cup buttermilk

½ cup grated Parmesan or Gruyère cheese

⅓ cup chopped black olives, to serve

Slow & Low Eggplant

This isn't pretty, but it's exceptionally tasty. Enjoy this intensely flavorful eggplant scooped over a bowl of rice or quinoa, mixed into a hearty pasta, or showered with chopped herbs. It's also nice as a filling for spring rolls or tacos or folded into a lettuce cup. In short, it's versatile. Use whatever dried mushrooms you have on hand; I tend to use porcini or chanterelle, but whatever you have will work.

6 cloves garlic

½ cup coarsely chopped shallots

1 tablespoon chopped dried mushrooms

¾ teaspoon fine-grain sea salt

¾ teaspoon red chile flakes

1 tomato, coarsely chopped

¼ teaspoon ground turmeric

3 tablespoons extra-virgin olive oil

8 ounces tempeh, crumbled

3 eggplants (1½ pounds in total), cut into ½-inch cubes

Lemon wedges and chopped mixed fresh herbs (cilantro, basil, mint), to serve

Combine the garlic, shallots, mushrooms, and salt in a mortar and pestle. Pound into a chunky paste. Alternately, you can pulse the ingredients in a blender. Stir in the chile flakes, tomato, and turmeric and pound a bit more. Set aside.

Place a large pot over medium-high heat. Add the oil, and when hot but not smoking, stir in the tempeh. Cook for a few minutes, until well browned. Stir in the garlic-tomato paste, then add the eggplant. Cover with a tight-fitting lid and dial back the heat to low. Cook, stirring every 6 to 7 minutes, until the eggplant collapses, 45 to 60 minutes. Resist the urge to add water if the pot seems dry; the eggplant will give off moisture toward the end.

Serve the eggplant topped with a big squeeze of lemon juice and lots of fresh herbs.

SERVES 4 TO 6

Variations

Add two big handfuls of chopped chard toward the end of cooking for an added boost of greens. Or add an equal amount of ricotta to the chard-eggplant mixture and use the filling to stuff pasta shells or dough for a calzone.

Red-Spiced Tempeh with Broccoli

Feisty and flavor-forward, this is my favorite kind of one-pan meal. The tempeh absorbs a boldly spiced chile-paprika tomato pan sauce that also pairs well with broccoli.

In a large, dry skillet over medium heat, toast the caraway and cumin seeds until fragrant, 1 to 2 minutes, and remove from heat.

Crush the seeds in a mortar and pestle, then transfer them to a small bowl along with the oil, red pepper flakes, paprika, and garlic. Stir to combine.

Add the garlic-spice mixture to the same skillet over medium-high heat and push it around the pan for 30 seconds, until fragrant. Add the tomato paste, lime juice, and salt and stir well. Add the water, continuing to stir, and bring to a simmer. Add the tempeh and broccoli. Cover and cook for 4 to 5 minutes, stirring once midway through. Once the broccoli is bright green and just-tender, remove the pan from the heat.

Scoop the mixture into bowls and top with a dollop of salted yogurt and a sprinkling of nuts.

SERVES 2 TO 4

1 tablespoon caraway seeds

1 tablespoon cumin seeds

2 tablespoons extra-virgin olive oil

½ teaspoon crushed red pepper flakes

2 teaspoons paprika

4 cloves garlic, smashed and chopped

¼ cup tomato paste

Juice of 1 lime

½ teaspoon fine-grain sea salt

1 cup water

8 ounces tempeh, crumbled

1 head broccoli, cut into small florets

Salted Garlic Yogurt (page 240) and toasted peanuts or almonds, to serve

7/
Sheet-Pan Meals

A Year of Pizzas & Flatbreads

I always keep balls of either homemade or store-bought pizza dough in my refrigerator, along with a few extras in the freezer, for quick weeknight meals. You can increasingly find whole wheat and whole grain versions. Here are some of my favorite combinations from the past year. If you're working with frozen dough, allow it to completely thaw and come to room temperature on a countertop before proceeding.

16 ounces Mixed Grain Dough (see recipe below) or store-bought whole wheat pizza dough

Preheat the oven to 450°F and place a rack in the center.

Rub a baking sheet with a bit of olive oil, and arrange the dough on top. Press it out until it covers the sheet in one even, thin layer, either in a circle like a pizza or in a more flatbread-like oval. Spread the sauce over the dough and add the toppings.

Bake for 7 to 10 minutes, until the crust is deeply golden. Finish with any drizzles and toppings.

SERVES 2 TO 4

Mixed Grain Dough

1 packet active dry yeast

½ cup warm water (110°F to 115°F)

½ teaspoon granulated cane sugar

1¼ cups rye flour

3 cups all-purpose flour

1 cup cold water

¾ cup cooked red or black quinoa

3 tablespoons extra-virgin olive oil, plus more as needed

1½ teaspoons fine grain sea salt

In the bowl of a stand mixer, whisk together the yeast, warm water, and sugar. Cover the bowl with a clean towel and let sit for about 15 minutes, until the mixture is puffy. This tells you the yeast is alive.

Stir in the flours, cold water, quinoa, 2 tablespoons of the oil, and the salt. Attach the dough hook to the stand mixer and knead the dough for 5 to 7 minutes, until it's stretchy and tacky. (Alternately, knead the dough with your hands on a well-floured countertop.) Turn the dough out onto a work surface. Wash the bowl and rub it with the remaining 1 tablespoon oil. Shape the dough into a ball and transfer it to the oiled bowl. Cover the bowl with a clean towel and let the dough rise in a warm place until doubled, typically 1 hour.

Punch the dough down, cut it into two pieces, and shape each into a ball. Rub with a bit more olive oil and place the balls on a plate or baking sheet until ready to use, or double wrap and refrigerate or freeze for up to 2 months.

MAKES 2 (16-OUNCE) DOUGH BALLS

Masala Flatbread

Tomato sauce (see page 235), seasoned with curry or chana masala spice blend

Chickpeas (lots of them)

Tiny cooked broccoli florets

Big dollops of plain Greek yogurt

Zest of 1 lemon

Crushed Crispy Curly Kale Chips (page 234) or chopped mixed fresh herbs and extra-virgin olive oil, to serve

Pesto & Artichoke Pizza

Thin layer of pesto

Chickpeas (lots of them)

Torn-up mozzarella balls or big dollops of plain Greek yogurt

Golden-Crusted Artichoke Hearts (page 69) and Magic Green Herby Drizzle (page 246), to serve

Loaded Veggie Flatbread

Thin layer of Magic Green Herby Drizzle (page 246), or your favorite pesto

Thick coins of cooked baby potatoes

Tiny cooked cauliflower florets

Raw curly kale leaves, tossed in a bit of extra-virgin olive oil

A generous amount of grated cheese of your choice

Fresh arugula tossed with extra-virgin olive oil and a bit of fine-grain sea salt, and lemon olive oil or extra-virgin olive oil with lots of lemon zest, to serve

Spring Pesto Pizza

Thin layer of pesto

Shelled and blanched fava beans or frozen peas

Sliced asparagus

Thinly sliced shallots or red onions

Big dollops of plain Greek yogurt

Crushed Crispy Curly Kale Chips (page 234) and more pesto, to serve

Harissa Flatbread

Thin layer of harissa

Chickpeas (lots of them)

Thinly sliced red onions

Oil-cured black olives, torn in half

Tiny cooked broccoli florets

Big dollops of plain Greek yogurt

Crushed Crispy Curly Kale Chips (page 234) and a drizzle of good extra-virgin olive oil, to serve

Spicy Chickpeas with Kale & Coconut

This combination of seasoned chickpeas, coconut, kale, quinoa, and avocado is quite good when bundled into a lettuce wrap if you have some bright, lively Little Gem lettuce around. Seek out curly-style kale here, since it crisps beautifully in the oven and use sesame-chile oil in place of toasted sesame oil if you like a bit of heat.

Preheat the oven to 375°F and place a rack in the center.

In a small bowl, whisk together the olive oil, sesame oil, and tamari.

Combine the kale, coconut, and yeast on a rimmed baking sheet and toss well using your hands (really go for it with the tossing!). Add about two-thirds of the oil mixture and toss again. Arrange the kale evenly across the baking sheet. Bake for 15 to 20 minutes, tossing once or twice along the way, until the kale is crisp and the coconut is deeply golden.

In the meantime, heat the chickpeas and quinoa in a small saucepan over medium heat. Transfer the warm chickpea-quinoa mixture to a serving bowl and toss with the remaining oil mixture.

Top the chickpeas with the kale-coconut mixture and place the avocado slices over the top. Serve warm with dollops of yogurt.

SERVES 4

¼ cup extra-virgin olive oil

1 teaspoon toasted sesame oil or sesame-chile oil

1½ tablespoons tamari or soy sauce

4 cups tightly packed chopped curly kale, stems trimmed and ribs removed

1 cup unsweetened shredded large-flake coconut

⅓ cup nutritional yeast

1 (15-ounce) can chickpeas, drained and rinsed

2 cups cooked quinoa or brown rice

1 ripe avocado, thinly sliced

Salted Garlic Yogurt (page 240), to serve (optional)

Golden Oven Fries with Dipping Sauces

These generous wedges with fluffy insides are everything you want in an oven fry. Use waxy new potatoes, sweet potatoes, or, even better, a mix of the two. My three favorite dipping sauces are here. I find that using a thick and creamy Greek yogurt for these dips gives a lovely rich texture.

1½ pounds waxy new potatoes, sweet potatoes, or a mix

2 tablespoons extra-virgin olive oil

⅛ teaspoon fine-grain sea salt

Place a baking sheet on the center rack of the oven and preheat the oven to 425°F.

Cut the potatoes into ½-inch-thick wedges. Place the wedges in a large bowl and toss with the oil and salt.

Carefully remove the hot baking sheet from the oven and arrange the wedges in a single layer. Bake for 25 to 35 minutes, flipping the potatoes once halfway through, until they are browned on both cut sides.

Transfer the potatoes to a platter and serve with one (or all!) of the dipping sauces.

SERVES 4

Dipping Sauces

SRIRACHA YOGURT: In a small bowl, whisk together 1 cup plain Greek yogurt, 1 to 2 tablespoons sriracha to taste, and ⅛ teaspoon fine-grain sea salt.

TURMERIC & BLACK PEPPER: In a small bowl, whisk together 1 cup plain Greek yogurt, 1 clove grated garlic, ¼ teaspoon ground turmeric, ¼ teaspoon freshly ground black pepper, and ⅛ teaspoon fine-grain sea salt.

HIBISCUS & GARLIC RAITA: In a small bowl, whisk together 1 cup plain Greek yogurt, 2 tablespoons minced shallots, 2 cloves grated garlic, and ⅛ teaspoon fine-grain sea salt. Sprinkle with ½ teaspoon dried hibiscus (jamaica), chopped into a chunky powder.

HARISSA KETCHUP: Season your favorite natural ketchup with harissa to taste.

Double-Crisp Potatoes with Salted Mustard Yogurt

Golden-crusted with fluffy interiors, these twice-roasted potatoes are wildly popular with kids and adults alike. Look for small potatoes—purple, pink, yellow, or a mix—not much longer than your thumb.

Preheat the oven to 425°F and place a rack in the center.

Place the potatoes and onions on a rimmed baking sheet. Drizzle the oil on top, sprinkle with the salt, and toss well. Arrange everything in a single layer and roast for 15 minutes. Toss the potatoes and onions again and roast for about 10 minutes more, removing the onions when browned and continuing to roast the potatoes until tender. Smash the potatoes with a fork and roast for 15 minutes more, flipping them once midway through, until deeply golden and crispy.

In the meantime, in a small bowl, whisk together the yogurt, mustard, and garlic. Taste and add a couple pinches of salt as needed. Spread the yogurt mixture across a serving plate, as an underdressing. Sprinkle the lentils across the yogurt. And, when ready, arrange the crispy potatoes and the onions on top. Toss the arugula with a small splash of oil and sprinkle it over the potatoes along with the pine nuts and a streak of mustard on the side. Serve it up family style.

SERVES 4

1 pound tiny potatoes, washed and well-dried

2 small yellow onions, sliced into ½-inch wedges

3 tablespoons extra-virgin olive oil, plus more to serve

¼ teaspoon fine-grain sea salt, plus more as needed

1 cup plain Greek yogurt

2 teaspoons Dijon-style mustard

2 cloves garlic, smashed into a paste

1 cup cooked black or French lentils (lentilles du Puy), warmed

2 handfuls of arugula

¼ cup toasted pine nuts

Whole-grain Dijon-style mustard, to serve

Roasted Chile-Peanut Tofu

This clean-out-the-fridge meal evolved into a regular go-to. It's admittedly a bit of a weirdo but in the best way. Use the firmest tofu you can find, either plain or your favorite marinated version. I call for preserved lemon because it lends a burst of brightness, but if you don't have any on hand, try making the Quick-Pickled Lemons (page 237)—they're such a fast cheat! Feel free to make the sauce a day or two ahead of time. Just store it in an airtight container in the fridge until you're ready to go. You can also toss a couple of handfuls of broccoli florets with a bit of olive oil and roast them with the tofu for some welcome green on your plate.

10 ounces extra-firm organic tofu

2 tablespoons extra-virgin olive oil

1½ tablespoons tamari or soy sauce

6 small cloves garlic, unpeeled

¼ teaspoon crushed red pepper flakes

¼ teaspoon fine-grain sea salt

1½ tomatoes, quartered

⅓ cup salted peanuts

6 black olives, pitted and slivered

1 tablespoon chopped preserved lemon (optional)

Lemon wedges and cooked brown rice or quinoa, to serve

Preheat the oven to 400°F and place a rack in the center.

Using a clean dish towel or paper towels, press as much moisture from the tofu as possible. Cut the tofu into bite-size chunks or slabs and place in a medium bowl along with 1 tablespoon of the oil and the tamari. Toss gently. Place the tofu chunks on a baking sheet and bake for 15 to 20 minutes, tossing once halfway through, until the tofu is deeply golden.

In the meantime, heat a large skillet over medium heat. Toast the garlic in its skins for 10 minutes, flipping now and then, until you see browning. Remove the pan from the heat and peel the garlic.

In a food processor or blender, combine the garlic, red pepper flakes, salt, tomatoes, and the remaining 1 tablespoon oil and puree until just smooth. Add the peanuts and pulse a few times, leaving them quite chunky. Transfer the mixture to a saucepan and stir in the olives and lemon. Warm the sauce over low heat, or, alternately, put it in an ovenproof dish and warm it up with the tofu in the oven.

Toss together the tofu and the warmed sauce in a medium bowl and serve with lemon wedges and brown rice or quinoa.

SERVES 4

Blistered Mushrooms with Croutons & Kale

An oven-roasted panzanella of sorts, this dish is a hearty assembly of toasted bread chunks, garlic-roasted mushrooms, and a medley of other flavor punctuations. I call this a double sheet-pan dish because it's made using multiple baking sheets in the same oven. You want to use either smallish, bite-size mushrooms or mushroom pieces. To clean the mushrooms, brush them with a damp towel. Enjoy this over soba or brown rice or alongside a poached egg. Give yourself bonus points for adding a big dollop of salted yogurt or sour cream on top.

Preheat the oven to 400°F and place the racks in the top and bottom third.

In a large bowl, combine the garlic, Parmesan, bread chunks, and lemon zest. Toss it a bit before adding the mushrooms, olives, 3 tablespoons of the oil, and the salt. Toss again and turn out the mixture onto a rimmed baking sheet, arranging everything in a single layer. Cover and carefully seal the baking sheet with aluminum foil.

Bake for 30 minutes on the bottom rack. Remove the foil (don't freak out; things will look a bit sad and steamed at this point) and bake for another 10 minutes or so, until everything is golden and toasted.

In the meantime, in a medium bowl, toss together the kale, the remaining 1 tablespoon oil, and the yeast. Arrange the mixture in a single layer on a second rimmed baking sheet and place it in the oven on the top rack. Bake for 10 minutes, tossing once halfway through, until the kale is crispy and not at all soggy.

To serve, scoop the mushrooms into a serving bowl and squeeze lemon juice over all. Crumble the baked kale on top along with a dollop of yogurt and a dusting of Parmesan.

SERVES 4

3 cloves garlic, chopped

½ cup grated Parmesan cheese, plus more to serve

1 cup whole grain bread, torn into tiny pieces

Zest and juice of 1 lemon

1 pound brown mushrooms, cleaned and halved

8 black olives, pitted and chopped

4 tablespoons extra-virgin olive oil

¼ teaspoon fine-grain sea salt

1 bunch kale, stemmed and ribs removed

3 tablespoons nutritional yeast

Salted Garlic Yogurt (page 240) or sour cream, to serve

Coconut-Baked Tofu with Broccoli & Beans

I love this cooking technique. You toss your main ingredients—in this case, tofu and vegetables—in a rich coconut and green curry milk, then cover, bake, and enjoy. Use the Cilantro–Green Curry Paste or a favorite store-bought green curry paste. And feel free to add a handful of green beans or cauliflower florets to the mix before roasting. Serve over cooked whole grain rice, quinoa, or farro.

1 cup well-mixed, full-fat coconut milk

3 tablespoons Cilantro–Green Curry Paste (page 256), or store-bought green curry paste

¼ teaspoon fine-grain sea salt

12 ounces extra-firm organic tofu

1 head broccoli, cut into florets

Generous handful of green beans, trimmed

1 lemon or lime, cut into 6 wedges

2 to 3 cups cooked brown rice or whole grains

Chopped cilantro, toasted nuts, and/or Serrano Chile Vinegar (page 240), to serve (optional)

Preheat the oven to 375°F and place a rack in the center.

In a small bowl, whisk together the coconut milk and curry paste. Season with the salt.

Cut the tofu into ½-inch cubes and combine them with the broccoli and green beans on a rimmed baking sheet. Alternately, use a 9 by 13-inch baking dish.

Pour the coconut-curry milk over the tofu and vegetables and toss well to combine. Nestle the citrus wedges into the mixture. Cover the baking dish with aluminum foil and bake for 15 to 20 minutes, until the broccoli is tender but not overcooked. Remove the foil and place under the broiler for a minute or two at the end of baking to give everything a bit of extra color. (Or, if you're not comfortable using your broiler, just leave the pan in the oven a big longer.)

Serve the curry over rice or whole grains, topped with a generous squeeze of baked citrus and plenty of fresh cilantro. A sprinkling of toasted nuts and a kiss of serrano vinegar is nice as well.

SERVES 4 TO 6

8/

Easy Grills

Grilled Rice Triangles

Yaki onigiri are simple Japanese grilled rice balls or triangles. Yaki means "rice," and onigiri means "grilled." You can tuck little fillings like tofu or edamame into their centers, then glaze them while they cook for a golden, slightly crusted and caramelized exterior. I use short-grain brown rice and a harissa-boosted glaze for mine. Grill these outside in the summer and opt for a skillet or griddle—preferably one that's well-seasoned cast iron—when it's too cold outside.

2 to 3 cups cold cooked short-grain brown rice

1 tablespoon harissa

2 tablespoons tamari or soy sauce

3 tablespoons white wine vinegar

3 tablespoons honey

Sliced green onions (white and tender green parts) and the zest of 1 lemon, to serve

Moisten your hands with cold water (to prevent sticking) and shape the rice into triangles (see photo). Alternately, shape the rice by pressing it into a container lined with plastic wrap or into an onigiri mold. Press the rice very firmly so it holds together, then set aside.

Preheat a grill to medium-high heat and brush the grates with oil to prevent sticking as needed.

In the meantime, in a small bowl, whisk together the harissa, tamari, vinegar, and honey.

Place the onigiri directly on the grates or on a griddle and grill each side until crisp and browned, a few minutes. Brush the largest sides of each onigiri with a bit of the glaze and grill for a few minutes more, until the glaze has caramelized a bit on both sides.

Serve the onigiri topped with green onions and lemon zest, with the remaining glaze on the side.

SERVES 4 TO 6

Grilled Corn Salad with Salty-Sweet Lime Dressing

Enjoy this salad at the peak of summer, preferably outdoors among friends and with an easy-drinking lager. The grilled corn is tossed with a serrano chile–spiked dressing that's a little bit sweet from brown sugar, just the right amount of sour from lime juice, and balanced overall by the saltiness of tamari. There's a nice crunch from toasted almonds, and cubes of avocado deliver the creaminess. You can make this dressing up to 3 days ahead of time and store it in an airtight container in the refrigerator.

Preheat a grill to medium-high heat.

Brush the corn with the oil. Grill the corn, turning the ears every couple of minutes, until the kernels are tender, 10 minutes or so. Remove the ears from the grill and let them cool. When they are cool enough to handle, cut off the kernels and place them in a medium serving bowl.

In the meantime, combine the tamari and brown sugar in a small saucepan over low heat. Simmer until the sugar dissolves and the sauce thickens a bit, about 3 minutes.

Remove the pan from the heat and pour the mixture into a blender. Add the lime juice, chiles, and garlic and blend until well combined. Alternately, add everything to the saucepan and combine using a hand blender.

Pour two-thirds of the dressing over the corn, add the cilantro and avocado, and toss gently. Taste and add more dressing as needed. Top with the almonds and serve.

SERVES 4 TO 6

4 ears husked corn

2 tablespoons extra-virgin olive oil

⅓ cup tamari or soy sauce

⅓ cup dark brown cane sugar

¼ cup freshly squeezed lime juice

2 serrano chiles, stemmed

3 cloves garlic

½ cup chopped cilantro leaves

1 ripe avocado, cubed

½ cup toasted sliced almonds

Grilled Romaine with Lemon-Buttermilk Dressing

For those days when you're going to grill *everything* you eat, this is your salad. I call for romaine lettuce (sometimes called romaine hearts), but any structured head of lettuce with a tight center and leaves (such as Little Gem, endive, or radicchio later in the year) will work. You want heads that will hold together nicely on the grill.

3 heads romaine lettuce

1 to 2 tablespoons extra-virgin olive oil

⅔ cup buttermilk

2 cloves garlic, grated

¼ cup plain Greek yogurt

Zest of 1 lemon

1 tablespoon freshly squeezed lemon juice

¼ teaspoon fine-grain sea salt

1 ripe avocado, sliced

⅓ cup toasted sliced almonds

Preheat a grill to medium-high heat.

Cut the romaine heads in half lengthwise and brush each with a bit of oil.

While the grill is heating, in a bowl, whisk together the buttermilk, garlic, yogurt, lemon zest and juice, and salt. Let the dressing sit for 10 to 15 minutes to develop the flavors.

When the grill is hot, add the lettuce, cut-side down, and grill just long enough to get a bit of char, 2 to 3 minutes. Transfer the romaine to a serving platter.

To serve, drizzle the romaine generously with the dressing and top each with avocado slices and nuts.

SERVES 6

Ratatouille on the Grill

One of my favorite ways to put a dent in summer produce is to make ratatouille. Many ratatouille recipes ask you to roast the veggies in an oven before bringing everything together on a stovetop. To beat the summer heat, I grill the eggplant and zucchini instead; this adds a nice charbroiled flavor to the dish. If you're worried about the vegetables falling through the grates, cut the pieces a bit larger or use grill baskets or a large grill pan.

1 eggplant (about 1 pound)

4 zucchini (about 2 pounds total)

8 tablespoons extra-virgin olive oil

Fine-grain sea salt

2 large yellow onions, chopped

¼ pound banana peppers, or any sweet peppers, stemmed

1½ pounds ripe tomatoes, chopped

½ teaspoon crushed red pepper flakes

5 cloves garlic, minced

½ cup water

1 cup chopped basil

Crushed saffron threads, smoked paprika, or grilled flatbread, to serve (optional)

Preheat a grill to medium-high heat.

Cut your eggplant and zucchini into ¾-inch pieces, keeping the two vegetables separate. Toss each pile with 2 tablespoons of the oil and a bit of salt.

Arrange the pieces in a single layer on the grill. Cook for 15 minutes or so, using a metal spatula to flip the veggies a few times along the way, until tender and golden. Remove the veggies from the grill and set aside.

On your stovetop, in your widest pot, heat the remaining 4 tablespoons oil over medium heat. Add the onions, peppers, and ½ teaspoon salt. Cook until soft and a bit translucent, 5 to 8 minutes. Stir in the tomatoes, red pepper flakes, garlic, and water. Simmer for 15 minutes or so, until the tomatoes are jammy and reduced.

Add the eggplant and zucchini to the pot, stir well, and simmer for a couple of minutes, until everything settles in together. Taste and add more salt as needed.

To serve, ladle the ratatouille into bowls and top with the basil. Add a big pinch of saffron, paprika to taste, or grilled flatbread on the side.

SERVES 6

Variation

To make a one-pot meal, drain and rinse a 15-ounce can of white beans and add them with the eggplant and zucchini.

Sesame-Nori Corn on the Cob

Keeping things simple yet interesting is how I like to approach peak summertime corn. Here, savory nutritional yeast melts into hot, butter-kissed corn, and the aroma of toasted nori, sesame, and lemon join the other scents coming off the grill. For a vegan version, brush with olive oil in place of butter.

Preheat a grill to medium-high heat.

Brush the corn with the butter and season with salt. Grill the corn, turning the ears every couple of minutes, until the kernels are tender and have some color, 10 minutes or so.

In the meantime, place the nori on the grill and toast until it crisps up and is easy to crumble, 1 to 2 minutes. Remove the nori from the grill and crumble it into a small bowl.

Place the grilled corn on a serving platter and shower it with the nori and yeast. Drizzle with the oil and finish with a sprinkling of sesame seeds and lemon zest.

SERVES 4

4 ears husked corn

2 tablespoons unsalted butter, melted

Fine-grain sea salt

2 (8-inch) sheets nori

⅓ cup nutritional yeast

1 tablespoon sesame-chile oil

2 tablespoons toasted sesame seeds

Lemon zest

Minted Mushroom Kebabs

I highlight one of my favorite dressings here, a refreshing date-studded and mint-flecked winner. It works well with the grilled notes of the mushrooms (see photo on page 188) but is equally delicious as a substitute dressing in the Lemony Carrot Salad (page 91) or spooned over Cheesy Lemon Pepper Polenta (opposite). And if you don't have dates on hand, well-chopped raisins are a perfectly good substitute. To clean the mushrooms, brush them with a damp towel.

1 pound mixed mushrooms (king trumpet, enoki, cremini, or your favorites)

½ cup extra-virgin olive oil

½ cup finely chopped mint leaves

2 small cloves garlic, smashed and minced

1 small shallot, minced

2 teaspoons pure maple syrup

2 tablespoons chopped dates

1 tablespoon grated Parmesan cheese

¼ teaspoon fine-grain salt

1 lemon

Preheat a grill to medium-high heat.

Cut the mushrooms into bite-size pieces, if necessary, and thread them evenly onto four kebab skewers. Brush the mushrooms with a bit of the oil.

In the meantime, in a small bowl, whisk together the remaining oil, the mint, garlic, shallot, maple syrup, dates, Parmesan, and salt. Set aside.

Place the kebabs on the grill and cook for 7 to 10 minutes, turning the kebabs a few times along the way, until evenly golden.

Transfer the kebabs to a serving platter, drizzle them generously with the dressing, and finish with a squeeze of lemon juice. Serve immediately.

SERVES 4

Cheesy Lemon Pepper Polenta

Flecked with black pepper and grilled, these polenta rounds (see photo on page 189) are dusted liberally with lemon zest and grated Parmesan. For some additional serving ideas, check out the variations below.

Preheat a grill to medium-high heat.

Slice the polenta into ½-inch-thick rounds, brush with the oil, and season with salt. Place the rounds on the grill and cook for 3 to 4 minutes, until golden and crusted. Flip and repeat on the other side.

Arrange the grilled polenta on a serving platter and sprinkle evenly with lemon zest, pepper, and cheese. Serve immediately.

SERVES 4

1 (18-ounce) tube polenta

Extra-virgin olive oil

Generous pinch of fine-grain sea salt

Zest of 2 lemons

½ teaspoon freshly ground black pepper

Grated Parmesan or Pecorino cheese (optional)

Variations

After grilling, instead of topping with lemon, pepper, and cheese, try this:

Shower with Magic Green Herby Drizzle (page 246).

Serve alongside Ratatouille on the Grill (page 186).

Finish with Oven-Roasted Cherry Tomatoes (page 236).

Summer Squash Mezze with Turmeric Oil

This summery dish works all season long: in June, I toss in segments of asparagus or artichoke hearts. As we head toward the fall, eggplant is a win. If you have a grill with narrow slats, you can throw the squash straight on it. Otherwise, use a grill basket so you don't lose pieces to the fire. And although I've given you a few suggestions here, feel free to use any of your favorite summer vegetables.

3 cloves garlic, minced

3 tablespoons extra-virgin olive oil

Scant ¼ teaspoon ground turmeric

⅛ teaspoon freshly ground black pepper, plus more to season

Fine-grain sea salt

1 cup plain Greek yogurt

1 (16-ounce) ball store-bought whole wheat pizza dough

Summer squash or zucchini (1½ pounds total), cut into bite-size pieces

1 cup cherry tomatoes or Oven-Roasted Cherry Tomatoes (page 236)

Preheat a grill to medium-high heat.

In a small stainless-steel bowl, combine half of the minced garlic with 2 tablespoons of the oil, the turmeric, pepper, and a pinch of salt. Set aside.

In a second small bowl, combine the remaining garlic with the yogurt and a pinch of salt and stir well. Set aside.

Divide the pizza dough into three equal pieces and gently shape each one into a ¼-inch-thick flatbread round. Arrange the flatbreads on the grill, close the top, and grill until the bottoms are golden, 2 to 3 minutes. Flip and grill the second sides in the same way, then remove the flatbreads from the heat to cool a bit. Cut them into wedges.

Place the squash in a bowl. Toss with the remaining 1 tablespoon oil and season with salt and pepper. Place the squash pieces on the grill and cook until golden and tender, 5 minutes or so.

Just before serving, warm the turmeric oil by placing it on the grill for a minute or so. Swoosh the yogurt in a thick slather across a serving platter. Arrange the squash, flatbread, and tomatoes over the yogurt and drizzle with the warmed turmeric oil.

SERVES 4 TO 6

9/
One-Bowl Bakes

Lemon-Millet Soda Bread

You can have the dough for this buttermilk-based soda bread made in under 5 minutes. It couldn't be easier, even for the most intimidated bakers. Surprise pops of millet and lemon zest lend brightness and texture. Slather it with a bit of salted butter or Turmeric-Coconut Ricotta (page 49).

2⅓ cups white whole wheat or rye flour

1¾ cups unbleached all-purpose flour, plus more to sprinkle

1¾ teaspoons baking soda

1¼ teaspoons fine-grain sea salt

8 tablespoons uncooked millet

Zest of 2 lemons

2 cups buttermilk, plus more to brush

Preheat the oven to 400°F and place a rack in the center.

In a large bowl, stir together the flours, baking soda, salt, 6 tablespoons of the millet, and the lemon zest. Pour in the buttermilk and stir until a dough forms. Knead the dough in the bowl or on a countertop for 30 seconds or so, until the dough comes together into a cohesive ball.

Lightly flour a baking sheet and place the dough on the sheet. Brush the top of the dough ball with buttermilk and sprinkle the top generously with about a tablespoon of flour. Slice across the top of the dough three times, creating pie-shaped wedges and cutting two-thirds of the way through the loaf. Sprinkle with the remaining 2 tablespoons millet.

Bake the dough for 30 to 35 minutes, until a hard crust forms and the bread is baked through. Cool on a wire rack before using. Wrap the bread and store it at room temperature for up to 2 days.

MAKES ONE 9-INCH LOAF

Big Raspberry-Rye Cookies

My wild card ingredient in these extra-large cookies is an entire bag of crushed freeze-dried raspberries. Paired with the rye flour, these cookies bake up crisp, golden, and vibrating with tart-sweet raspberry intensity. If you find the size to be intimidating, go ahead and cut them into quarters to serve on a cookie plate. The dough also freezes really well, shaped into balls and double wrapped, for up to 2 months. But if you're going to bake from frozen, increase the baking time by 4 to 6 minutes.

195g ¾ cup plus 2 tablespoons room-temperature unsalted butter, sliced

250g 1½ cups granulated cane sugar

50g ¼ cup dark brown cane sugar

1 egg

2 teaspoons vanilla extract

290g 2¼ cups rye flour

½ teaspoon baking soda

½ teaspoon fine-grain sea salt

1 cup freeze-dried raspberries, crushed

Preheat the oven to 350°F and place a rack in the top third. Line two baking sheets with parchment paper.

Place the butter in a large bowl and beat it by hand or with an electric mixer until light and fluffy. Add the sugars and beat until uniform. Stir in the egg and vanilla extract until well combined. Add the flour, then sprinkle with the baking soda, salt, and raspberries. Stir just until the dough is combined.

Using a ¼-cup measure, form the dough into twelve balls. Place six balls on each prepared baking sheet and chill the dough in the freezer for 15 minutes before baking. You could also chill the dough in the refrigerator overnight.

Bake the cookies one pan at a time for 15 to 18 minutes, until the edges are deeply golden. Remove the pans from the oven and transfer the cookies to a wire rack to cool completely. Store in a cookie jar.

MAKES 12 COOKIES

Variations

BIG BLUEBERRY-WALNUT RYE COOKIES:
Replace the raspberries with crushed freeze-dried blueberries and add 1 cup chopped walnuts to the flour mixture.

BIG BANANA, COCO-CHIP RYE COOKIES:
Replace the raspberries with chopped freeze-dried banana chips. Add 1 cup unsweetened shredded large-flake coconut to the flour mixture, along with 1 cup chocolate chips or ½ cup cacao nibs.

BIG SEED RYE COOKIES: Omit the raspberries and replace the vanilla extract with 2 teaspoons almond extract. Stir ½ cup mixed seeds (sesame, hemp, chia, etc.) into the flour mixture. Roll the dough balls in another ½ cup mixed seeds before placing them on parchment-lined baking sheets (see photo on page 202).

BIG WHOLE WHEAT COOKIES: Replace the rye flour with whole wheat flour and use whatever freeze-dried berries you like.

Nutritional Yeast Biscuits

I use nutritional yeast—packed with B vitamins, folate, and protein—to add a healthy boost to everything from nut butters to salads to these feathery biscuits. It lends a cheesy note and doubles down on the savory. These beauties are best served hot and slathered with your favorite spread (there are lots of ideas on pages 252 to 254) or drizzled with great extra-virgin olive oil.

Place a baking sheet on the center rack of the oven and preheat the oven to 450°F.

In a food processor fitted with the standard blade, pulse together the flours, yeast, salt, and baking powder once or twice. Sprinkle the butter cubes across the dry ingredients and pulse fifteen to twenty times, until the mixture resembles tiny pebbles. Add the yogurt and pulse just two or three times more; avoid overmixing the dough.

Gather the dough into a ball and turn it out onto a lightly floured surface. Knead the dough five times and press it into a 1-inch-thick square. Cut the square in half and stack one piece on top of the other. Flatten the dough into a 1-inch-thick square again and repeat the cutting and stacking. Repeat this process one more time, then press or roll the dough into a ¾-inch-thick rectangle. Cut the dough into twelve square biscuits and brush the tops with egg.

Carefully remove the hot baking sheet from the oven. Transfer the biscuits to the baking sheet, leaving ½ inch between each biscuit. Bake for 15 to 18 minutes, until the bottoms are deeply golden and the biscuits are cooked through. Serve immediately.

Wrap leftover biscuits and store them at room temperature for up to 2 days. Toast or reheat in a warm oven to serve.

MAKES 12 BISCUITS

1¼ cups rye flour

1 cup unbleached all-purpose flour, plus more to sprinkle

⅓ cup nutritional yeast

1½ teaspoons fine-grain sea salt

1 tablespoon aluminum-free baking powder

½ cup cold unsalted butter, cut into tiny cubes

1⅓ cups plain Greek yogurt

1 egg, whisked

Sunflower Brittle

This sheet-pan brittle is the perfect little bite when you need a sweet treat. But don't limit yourself to that. Because it is super crunchy, a little bit spicy, and a tad salted, you can scatter broken pieces across savory salads and breakfast bowls as well. Feel free to replace up to half of the sunflower seeds with sesame seeds, pepitas, peanuts, almonds, or a combination.

2 cups raw sunflower seeds

½ teaspoon cayenne pepper

½ teaspoon fine-grain sea salt

⅓ cup pure maple syrup

Preheat the oven to 325°F and place a rack in the center. Line a baking sheet with parchment paper.

Combine the seeds, cayenne, salt, and maple syrup in a bowl and mix until the seeds are completely coated. Pour the mixture into the center of the prepared baking sheet and use a spoon to press it out into an even ¼-inch-thick layer.

Bake for about 25 minutes, until the edges are deeply golden. Remove from the oven and let the brittle cool completely; it will crisp as it cools.

Smack the baking sheet on the counter to break the brittle into shards. If your brittle isn't breaking up, put it back in the oven for 10 minutes more, then cool and try again. Once the brittle is absolutely, completely cool, it will keep in an airtight container at room temperature for up to a month.

MAKES ½ POUND OF BRITTLE

Variations

Turmeric, Black Pepper & Pepita Brittle: Replace 1 cup sunflower seeds with pepitas and add ¼ teaspoon each ground turmeric and freshly ground black pepper.

Pho-Spiced Sunflower Brittle: Replace the cayenne with an all-natural pho spice blend (typically a combination of star anise, cinnamon, cloves, and ginger).

Easy Olive Oil Cake

Made with 100 percent rye flour, this cake is moist, rustic, shot through with berries, and endlessly adaptable. It's good the day after you make it and the day after that.

1 cup extra-virgin olive oil

3 eggs

¾ cup dairy, almond, or oat milk, or other favorite milk

2¼ cups rye flour

1 cup granulated cane sugar

1½ teaspoons aluminum-free baking powder

½ teaspoon fine-grain sea salt

1 (1-ounce) bag freeze-dried berries (raspberries, strawberries, blueberries, or a blend)

Preheat the oven to 350°F and place a rack in the center. Grease an 8-inch cake pan with 1 teaspoon of the oil.

In a large wide bowl, whisk together the remaining oil, the eggs, and milk. Sprinkle the flour, ¾ cup of the sugar, the baking powder, and salt over the top of the wet ingredients. Use a spatula to mix until barely combined. Sprinkle the berries over the top and stir a few times more. Pour the batter into the prepared pan and spread it evenly. Sprinkle the top with the remaining ¼ cup sugar.

Bake the cake for 30 to 40 minutes, until the top is golden brown and a skewer inserted into the center comes out clean. Serve the cake warm from the pan or transfer it to a wire rack to cool. The cake will keep, covered, in the refrigerator for up to 5 days. Bring it to room temperature before serving.

MAKES ONE 8-INCH CAKE

California Blender Cookies

I carry a few of these bite-size cookies in my purse when I'm traveling or facing a long day of work. They are what I like to call semi-virtuous, featuring oatmeal, peanut butter, and (wildcard!) chickpeas or white beans. They're free of refined sugar, studded with chocolate, and packed with nuts and seeds, and the combination of maple syrup and peanut butter is magic.

Preheat the oven to 350°F and place a rack in the center. Line two baking sheets with parchment paper.

Place the walnuts and oats in a blender or food processor and pulse into a flour. Add the chickpeas to the blender along with the maple syrup, peanut butter, vanilla, salt, and baking soda. Blend until smooth. Use a wooden spoon to stir in the chia seeds and chocolate chips.

One tablespoon at a time, shape the dough into balls and place them on the prepared baking sheets 1 inch apart. Bake for 10 to 12 minutes, in batches as needed, until golden. Transfer the cookies to a wire rack to cool. The cookies will keep in an airtight container in the refrigerator for up to a week.

MAKES 24 COOKIES

¾ cup walnuts

1 cup old-fashioned rolled oats

1 (15-ounce) can chickpeas or white beans, drained and rinsed

⅓ cup pure maple syrup

⅔ cup all-natural peanut butter

2 teaspoons vanilla extract

½ teaspoon fine-grain sea salt

1 teaspoon baking soda

⅓ cup chia seeds

½ cup bittersweet chocolate chips

Variations

Cacao Nib Cookies: Roll each ball of dough in cacao nibs and bake as directed.

Toasted Turmeric-Coconut Cookies: Combine ⅓ cup unsweetened shredded large-flake coconut with ¼ teaspoon ground turmeric. Roll each ball of dough in the mixture and bake as directed.

Berry-Dusted Cookies: Use a mortar and pestle to crush ¼ cup freeze-dried raspberries or strawberries into a fine powder. Sprinkle the berry dust over the cookies after baking.

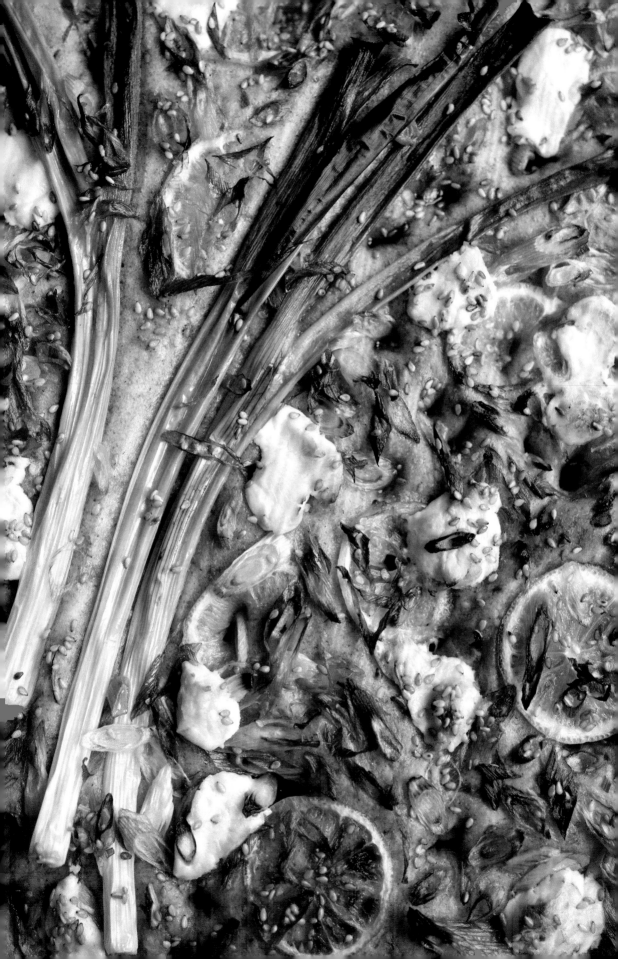

Rustic Focaccia

This is the base recipe for a beautiful focaccia that you can top in endless ways. If you're nervous about working with yeast dough, this is your gateway bread. I use a blend of rye and all-purpose flours, but if you want to use 100 percent whole grain flours, use white whole wheat flour instead of the all-purpose flour. It will be denser but still delicious, especially served hot from the oven.

1½ cups warm water (110°F to 115°F)

1 packet active dry yeast

1 teaspoon granulated cane sugar or honey

2¼ cups all-purpose flour

1¼ cups rye flour

1 teaspoon fine-grain sea salt, plus more to sprinkle

4 tablespoons extra-virgin olive oil

Pour the water into a large bowl and sprinkle in the yeast and sugar. Let it sit for 5 minutes or so, until it gets foamy.

Add the flours, salt, and 1 tablespoon of the oil. Using a wooden spoon, mix until the dough comes together, then turn it out onto a work surface. Wash the bowl, rub it with another 1 tablespoon of the oil, and set it aside.

Knead the dough for 5 minutes or so, until it feels smooth and elastic. Return the dough to the bowl, turning it in the oil. Cover the bowl with a clean dish towel and let it rise in a warm place until doubled, typically 1 hour.

In the meantime, preheat the oven to 400°F and place a rack in the center.

Tip the dough into an 8 by 12-inch baking dish or onto a baking sheet to bake it free-form and deflate it across the pan with flat hands. Let it rise, covered, for another 20 to 30 minutes, until the dough is nice and puffy.

Use your fingers to press lots of deep holes into the dough. Drizzle the remaining 2 tablespoons oil over the dough and sprinkle with a bit more salt. Bake for 20 minutes, until the focaccia is deeply golden and cooked through. Transfer the bread to a wire rack to cool for a bit before cutting. Taste and sprinkle with a bit more salt as needed.

Wrap the focaccia and store it at room temperature for up to 2 days. Make croutons or bread crumbs after that.

MAKES ONE 8 BY 12-INCH LOAF

Variations

SESAME–GREEN ONION FOCACCIA
(see photo on pages 214 and 215): Add ¼ cup
toasted sesame seeds along with the flours.
Top with whole and chopped green onions (white
and tender green parts), a few whisper-thin slices
of lemon, ⅓ cup crumbled goat cheese, and
1 tablespoon sesame seeds after flattening the
dough into the pan.

SUNFLOWER FOCACCIA: Make a seed blend
by lightly crushing 1 tablespoon dill seeds and
¼ cup sunflower seeds in a mortar and pestle. Stir
in 2 tablespoons hemp seeds and ½ tablespoon
dill pollen. Stir two-thirds of this mixture into the
flour mixture and sprinkle the remaining one-third
on top before baking.

ORANGE–PINE NUT FOCACCIA: After
flattening the dough into the pan, top with
½ orange, sliced razor thin; 12 pitted and halved
olives; and ¼ cup pine nuts.

HEMP-ROSEMARY FOCACCIA: After
flattening the dough into the pan, add ¼ cup
hemp seeds, 2 tablespoons chopped rosemary,
2 tablespoons chopped thyme, and 4 cloves
chopped garlic. Top with 2 Meyer lemons, sliced
razor thin; 15 pitted and halved black olives; and
¼ cup sliced almonds.

10/

Easy-Drinking Refreshers

Sunset Goji Nectar

Pureed dried goji berries make an antioxidant-rich juice that is slightly tart and sweet at the same time. Blended with coconut water, they also make one of the prettiest drinks I've seen. Consider spiking this nectar with tequila or use sparkling wine in place of the coconut water for a boozy brunch.

½ cup goji berries, soaked overnight

2 cups unsweetened coconut water

Ice cubes, to serve

Freshly squeezed orange juice or blood orange juice

Drain the goji berries. Transfer them to a high-speed blender, add the coconut water, and process until uniform and smooth. Strain and serve over ice with a generous squeeze of citrus juice on top.

SERVES 4

Matcha Seltzer

Stonemill Matcha is a matcha-centric café in San Francisco's Mission District, and the first place I encountered bubbly seltzer matcha. I loved the refreshing lightness, and I now make versions of it at home. Seek out good-quality matcha; it's worth the splurge. And be sure to serve this extra cold over lots of ice cubes.

In a pitcher, whisk the matcha with a splash of the sparkling water. Keep going until the mixture is smooth and frothy. Add the rest of the sparkling water, then pour the mixture into tall glasses filled with ice cubes.

SERVES 2

1 teaspoon matcha powder

1 (12-ounce) can sparkling water or seltzer, Coconut LaCroix, or Grapefruit Spindrift

Ice cubes, to serve

Jasmine Tea Sparkler

The night before your next brunch, brew your favorite jasmine tea and chill it. It's the secret ingredient in this fragrant, effervescent batch of gingery bubbles.

12 ounces strong ginger beer

1 bottle Prosecco

1 cup iced jasmine tea

Ice cubes, to serve (optional)

Combine the ginger beer, Prosecco, and jasmine tea in a punch bowl or decorative pitcher. Serve well chilled or over ice.

SERVES 6

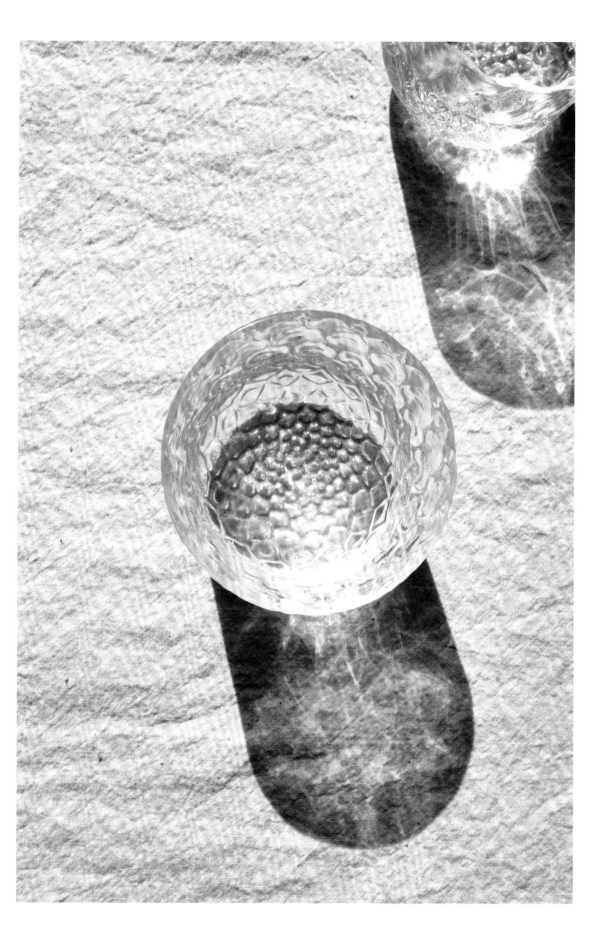

This lovely lassi-style quencher is perfect for an outdoor meal. This version uses grapefruit juice, orange blossom water, and a yogurt base, but you can play around with the ingredients. Try orange or blood orange juice or a blend of citrus juices. Rose water is really nice, too.

Combine the yogurt, grapefruit juice, orange blossom water, vanilla, and salt in a jar or pitcher. Taste and add more orange blossom water as needed and a thread of honey. Serve over lots of ice.

SERVES 2

1 cup plain Greek yogurt

⅓ cup freshly squeezed grapefruit juice

½ teaspoon orange blossom water, plus more to taste

½ teaspoon vanilla or almond extract

Pinch of fine-grain sea salt

Honey, to taste (optional)

Ice cubes, to serve

Dragon Fruit Shrub

When you come across dragon fruit (pitaya) puree in the freezer section, don't pass it up because you're going to want to make this shrub. Its sweetness is balanced with acidity from the vinegar and melon notes from the dragon fruit. Although it takes about a week for the flavors to mellow and come together, it keeps for weeks in the refrigerator. A splash in seltzer water, Prosecco, or even salad dressing is electric.

2 (3.5-ounce) packets frozen dragon fruit

1½ cups granulated cane sugar

1 cup apple cider vinegar or white wine vinegar

Sparkling water or Prosecco, to serve

Place the dragon fruit in a sterilized quart-size jar with a lid.

Combine the sugar and vinegar in a small saucepan over medium heat. Bring it to a simmer and stir to dissolve the sugar. Pour this hot mixture over the dragon fruit and stir well. Close the jar and store it in a cool, dark place for 5 days. Stored in the jar in the fridge, this mixture will keep for about a month.

To serve, stir 1 tablespoon into a glass of sparkling water or Prosecco. Taste and add more to your liking.

MAKES 2 CUPS

These coconut water teas give you a nice boost of potassium. I use a 1:1 ratio of tea to coconut water, but that's more personal preference than anything. Add a tablespoon of chia seeds for added texture.

Oolong-Coco Tea

Fill a tall glass with ice, add equal parts iced oolong tea and unsweetened coconut water and a giant squeeze of fresh lemon juice.

Hibiscus-Coco Tea

Fill a tall glass with ice, add equal parts iced hibiscus tea and unsweetened coconut water and a giant squeeze of fresh lime juice.

The Fade–Coco Tea

Fill a tall glass with ice, add iced oolong tea until the glass is half full. Add some unsweetened coconut water and gently top it off with strong hibiscus tea to create a beautiful gradient.

Makrut Lime & Green Iced Tea

Because of its big flavor, versatility, and exceptional aromatics, makrut lime is one of my favorite ingredients, so much so that I planted a tree in our yard. Although it is native to Southeast Asia, many people grow them in the United States. Check citrus vendors at your local farmers' market. The leaves freeze well, so when you find them, stock up. In this iced green tea, the lime is wonderfully fragrant. If you don't brew loose tea, toss the leaves into the pot along with a bag of green tea; fish out the leaves before sipping.

2 cups water

1 teaspoon loose green tea or 1 green tea bag

2 makrut lime leaves, crumbled and torn

Ice cubes, to serve

Heat the water in a small pan over medium-high heat until just shy of boiling. Add the tea and lime leaves and brew for 2 to 3 minutes or to taste. Let it steep for more time if you like a stronger flavor. Strain the tea into a pitcher and put it in the fridge to chill. Serve over ice.

MAKES 2 CUPS

Iced Hibiscus Cooler

Hibiscus is one of the most antioxidant-rich teas you can drink. Brew it strong along with turmeric and ginger, and you have a real powerhouse quencher. This trio is also a favorite prepared hot, whenever I feel a cold coming on. Note that turmeric stains intensely, so keep it away from anything you wouldn't want to turn bright yellow.

Fill a pot or teakettle with water and bring it to a boil over high heat.

In the meantime, slice the turmeric and ginger paper thin. Place the turmeric, ginger, and hibiscus flowers in a teapot, add the hot water, and brew for 2 to 3 minutes or to taste. Let it steep for more time if you like a stronger flavor. Strain the tea into a pitcher and put it in the fridge to chill. Serve over ice.

SERVES 2 TO 4

½-inch piece fresh turmeric, peeled

1-inch piece fresh ginger, peeled

1 tablespoon dried hibiscus (jamaica) flowers

Ice cubes, to serve

Toasted Coconut Milk

I posted this recipe to my website a few years ago, and people went crazy for it. If you love coconut milk, this is an intensely creamy, rich, nutty version. You can use it in chai, curries, ice creams, and baked oatmeal—basically, anytime coconut milk is called for in a recipe. Be sure to toast your coconut well if you want the flavor to be extra pronounced, but be mindful that the coconut can go from golden to burned in a flash, so set a timer. Also, like all pure coconut milks, this will separate and solidify in the refrigerator. Use it as you would canned coconut milk and expect it to behave similarly (for example, you might need to warm it up and give it a good stir before using).

1½ cups unsweetened shredded large-flake coconut

4 cups water

Fine-grain sea salt

Pure maple syrup or liquid stevia, to taste (optional)

Preheat the oven to 350°F and place a rack in the center.

Spread the coconut flakes in an even layer on a baking sheet. Bake for 7 to 10 minutes, flipping the flakes once along the way, until toasted and golden. Remove the baking sheet from the oven and let the toasted flakes cool.

In a blender, combine the coconut, water, and salt to taste. Blend and then blend some more, until smooth. Pour the milk through a nut bag (this makes it so easy!) or fine-mesh strainer into a quart-size jar with a lid. Sweeten with maple syrup to taste. Stored in the refrigerator, the milk will keep for up to 5 days.

MAKES ABOUT 1 QUART

Power Pantry

BASICS

You may recognize a couple of these recipes. Some of them, like the Five-Minute Tomato Sauce (opposite page) and Oven-Roasted Cherry Tomatoes (page 236) have been included in my other books. These are the little recipes that don't fit in another chapter but are indispensably part of my everyday cooking.

Crispy Curly Kale Chips

1 bunch curly kale, stems trimmed and ribs removed

1½ tablespoons extra-virgin olive oil

¼ cup nutritional yeast

Scant ⅛ teaspoon fine-grain sea salt

The rule around here is simple: if the oven is on for any reason, make a batch (or two) of these kale chips. They're great straight off the pan and also make the perfect super-green finishing touch to all manner of things. Crush over just-baked flatbreads or add them as a crunchy salad topping or to finish your favorite noodle bowl. The key here is to use curly kale. And after washing it, make sure it is completely dry. If there's residual water on the leaves, they'll steam instead of crisp. Be sure to keep your eye on the kale while it's baking; the only thing I burn more than kale chips is pine nuts.

Preheat the oven to 375°F and place a rack in the center.

Tear the kale into bite-size pieces. You should end up with about 3 ounces, or enough to cover a baking sheet in a single layer.

Transfer the kale to a large bowl and toss it well with the oil, yeast, and salt. Really get in there and massage the kale.

Arrange the kale on a baking sheet or two as needed to make a uniform layer. Bake for 15 to 17 minutes, flipping the kale once after 10 minutes, until the kale has crisped up nicely. Let the kale cool completely on the baking sheet for maximum crunch. Store it in a jar with a lid or another airtight container at room temperature for up to a week.

MAKES 4 CUPS

Five-Minute Tomato Sauce

¼ cup extra-virgin olive oil

1½ teaspoons crushed red pepper flakes

½ teaspoon fine-grain sea salt, plus more to taste

3 cloves garlic, finely chopped

1 (28-ounce) can crushed red tomatoes

Zest of 1 lemon

This sauce is as simple as it comes: bright and clear with straight tomato flavor accented by the right amount of red pepper flakes and garlic. Use this sauce on pizza, flatbreads, and pastas or as a jumping-off point for countless other recipes. If you stir in a tablespoon of a favorite curry powder, you can use the sauce on an Indian-spiced flatbread. Add a tablespoon of your favorite red curry paste and ¼ cup coconut milk and you change the sauce entirely. Play around!

Combine the oil, red pepper flakes, salt, and garlic in a cold saucepan. Stir while you heat the saucepan over medium-high heat and sauté for 45 seconds or so, until everything is fragrant—you don't want the garlic to brown. Stir in the tomatoes and heat to a gentle simmer, about 2 minutes. Remove the pan from the heat and carefully have a taste. If the sauce needs more salt, add it now. Stir in the lemon zest, reserving a bit to sprinkle on top of your pasta.

MAKES 4 CUPS

French Onion Salt

¼ cup dried minced onion

1 tablespoon onion powder

1 teaspoon garlic powder

½ teaspoon fine-grain sea salt

3 tablespoons chopped dried chives

This blend gives the French Onion Breakfast Strata (page 50) its distinctive flavor profile. Chives are my herb of choice, but oregano or thyme is also nice. This salt pairs well with baked sweet potatoes and is delicious sprinkled on Lemon-Millet Soda Bread (page 198) or Nutritional Yeast Biscuits (page 205).

In a jar with a lid, combine the minced onion, onion powder, garlic powder, salt, and chives. Store the salt at room temperature for up to 6 months.

MAKES ½ CUP

Nori-Peanut Crunch

2 (8-inch) sheets nori

¾ teaspoon crushed red pepper flakes

1 cup salted peanuts, chopped

2 tablespoons nutritional yeast

Zest of 1 lemon

This topping can be sprinkled on grain and noodle bowls or on savory oatmeal.

Preheat the oven to 350°F and place a rack in the center.

Place the nori on a baking sheet and toast until crispy, 4 to 5 minutes. Remove the nori from the oven, let them cool a bit, and then crumble into a small bowl. Add the red pepper flakes, peanuts, yeast, and zest to the bowl and mix well. Store in a jar with a lid at room temperature for up to a month.

MAKES ⅓ CUP

Oven-Roasted Cherry Tomatoes

1 pint cherry tomatoes

¼ cup extra-virgin olive oil, plus more to top

1 tablespoon pure maple syrup or dark brown cane sugar

Scant ½ teaspoon fine-grain sea salt

I nearly always have these tomatoes on hand, particularly during tomato season. Roast cherry tomatoes until deeply caramelized and store them in a jar with a glug of olive oil. The list of dishes I like them on is long: Avocado–Kale Chip Toast (page 43), Cheesy Lemon Pepper Polenta (page 191), Summer Squash Mezze with Turmeric Oil (page 192), all manner of pizzas and flatbreads (see page 162; add the tomatoes when the dough comes out of the oven), and even waffles, when we do a savory waffle night.

Preheat the oven to 350°F and place a rack in the top third.

Slice each tomato in half and place them in a large baking dish or on a rimmed baking sheet.

In a small bowl, whisk together the oil, maple syrup, and salt. Pour the mixture over the tomatoes and gently toss until well coated. Arrange the tomatoes cut-side up and roast for 45 to 60 minutes, until the tomatoes shrink a bit and start to caramelize around the edges. If you aren't using immediately, let the tomatoes cool, then scrape them into a clean jar along with any oil left in the dish. Sometimes I top off the jar with an added splash of oil. The tomatoes will keep for about 1 week in the refrigerator.

MAKES I CUP

Pickled Turmeric

1 cup apple cider vinegar

¼ cup white or brown granulated cane sugar

1 teaspoon fine-grain sea salt

1 shallot, thinly sliced

2 small serrano chiles, seeded and halved

1 cup peeled and thinly sliced fresh turmeric

Earthy, tangy, and electric yellow-orange in color, this pickled turmeric is just what you need to add drama to your grain bowls and salads. The pickling liquid won't be as pretty if you use brown cane sugar or coconut sugar; regular white sugar lets the turmeric yellow shine through. Basically, any granulated sugar will work here.

In a small saucepan over medium heat, combine the vinegar, sugar, and salt and simmer, stirring, until the sugar dissolves. Place the shallot, chiles, and turmeric in a pint jar with a lid. Pour the vinegar mixture over the ingredients in the jar. Store in the refrigerator for up to a month.

MAKES I CUP

Quick-Pickled Lemons

1 lemon

½ teaspoon fine-grain sea salt

White wine vinegar

No one wants to buy a jar of preserved lemons just for one recipe. I came up with this variation in a pinch one night and have been using it ever since. Similar to traditionally preserved lemons, these pickled lemons add a salty, bright, tangy punctuation to any bowl or salad.

With a sharp knife, trim the rind from the lemon and set aside the flesh. Mince the rind into small confetti-shaped flecks and transfer to a small jar with a lid. Stir in the salt and then top the rind with as much lemon juice as you can squeeze from the flesh, being mindful not to get any seeds in the jar. Top off the jar with a splash of vinegar to ensure the lemon rind is covered. Let everything sit for 15 minutes before using or store in the refrigerator for up to 2 weeks.

Variation

Stir in ¼ teaspoon lightly crushed fennel seeds and ¼ teaspoon ground turmeric.

MAKES ABOUT ½ CUP

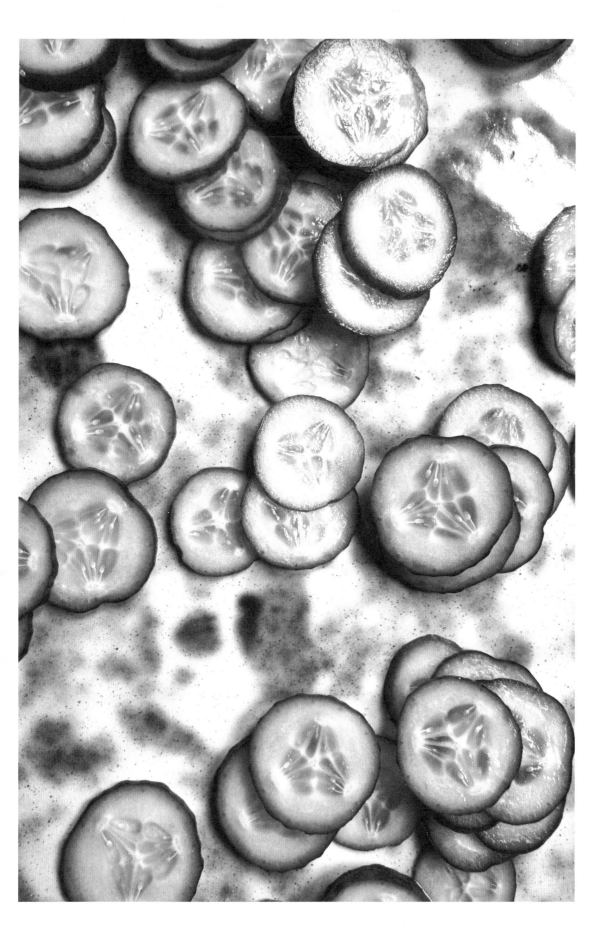

Serrano Chile Vinegar

8 serrano chiles, seeded and
sliced ⅛ inch thick

2 cups white vinegar

Top your tacos with this vinegar and some of the chiles used to make
it. You also can't go wrong by spiking your noodle bowls with the same.

Combine the chiles and vinegar in a pint-size jar with a lid. Store,
covered, in the refrigerator. Use the chiles within 2 weeks and the
vinegar within 4 weeks.

MAKES 2 CUPS

Salted Garlic Yogurt

2 cloves garlic

¼ teaspoon fine-grain sea salt

1 cup plain Greek yogurt

This is the condiment I reach for more than just about any other. It
adds a creamy component that works with everything from sheet-pan
dishes, such as Spicy Chickpeas with Kale & Coconut (page 167), to
burritos and flatbreads (see page 162), to Ten-Ingredient Masala Chili
(page 114). You can dial up or down the garlic to taste.

Place the garlic on a cutting board and sprinkle the salt on top. Using
the side of a sharp knife, cut and mash the garlic and salt into a paste.
Scoop the paste into a jar with a lid and stir in the yogurt. Store the
salted yogurt in the refrigerator for up to 3 days.

MAKES I CUP

BROTHS

You can do endless things with a great-tasting broth: Add a few pot stickers (see page 156) and you have a meal. Stir in a bit of miso, and you've got your own unique take on miso soup. Ladle it over your favorite noodles, use it in a risotto, or just sip it at mealtimes. Spicy broths are my favorites; they lend an invigorating jolt to just about any meal.

I make a lot of soups utilizing the following formula: sauté a few aromatics, add one or two main hero ingredients, and finish with filtered water or homemade broth as the base. Keeping the combination simple allows the main ingredient to shine through. And you can change the personality of a soup depending on the broth you choose. I've included some favorites in this section.

Black Garlic Broth

4 quarts water

½ cup dried porcini mushrooms

12 cloves black garlic

2 teaspoons crushed red pepper flakes

2 teaspoons fine-grain sea salt, plus more to taste

Fermented black garlic can be found in many stores or ordered online, and it is well worth tracking down. It has an unctuous datelike texture with a completely distinct flavor of soy sauce, dates, and subtle garlic notes. It makes a beautiful broth.

Add the water to a large stockpot over high heat. While the water is coming to a boil, add the mushrooms, black garlic, and red pepper flakes. Once the broth comes to a boil, reduce the heat and simmer for 30 minutes. Season with the salt, adding more as needed. Pour the broth through a fine-mesh strainer into an airtight container. The broth will keep for up to 5 days in the refrigerator or up to 3 months in the freezer.

MAKES 3 QUARTS

Favorite Mushroom Broth

4 quarts water

1 cup dried porcini or
portobello mushrooms

1 head garlic

2 teaspoons fine-grain sea salt,
plus more to taste

1 teaspoon freshly ground
black pepper, plus more to taste

Chopped thyme leaves

This broth is incredibly simple—using only mushrooms, pepper, garlic, salt, and thyme—but it makes a wonderful base for risotto, congee, or many broth pasta bowls.

Add the water to a large stockpot over high heat. While the water is coming to a boil, add the mushrooms. Smash each garlic clove to remove the peels and add the cloves to the pot. Once the broth comes to a boil, reduce the heat and simmer for 30 minutes. Season with the salt and pepper, adding more as needed. Serve hot, strained or not, sprinkled with lots of fresh thyme. The broth will keep in an airtight container for up to 5 days in the refrigerator or up to 3 months in the freezer.

MAKES 3 QUARTS

Lime-Leaf Broth

4 quarts water

12 makrut lime leaves, crumbled

4 lemongrass stalks, trimmed
and crushed

½ teaspoon fine-grain sea salt

2 serrano chiles, seeded and
halved

1 head garlic

¼ cup tamari or soy sauce, plus
more to taste

2-inch piece fresh ginger, peeled

1 or 2 limes

This is one of my favorite bases for brothy noodle bowls and curries.

Add the water to a large stockpot over high heat. While the water is coming to a boil, add the lime leaves, lemongrass, salt, and chiles. Smash each garlic clove and add them to the pot along with the tamari. Slice the ginger into ¼-inch-thick coins, smash them a bit, and add to the pot. Once the broth comes to a boil, reduce the heat and simmer for 15 minutes. Remove the pot from the heat and let it cool a bit. Taste and add more tamari as needed for saltiness. Finish with big squeezes of lime juice until the broth tastes vibrant and balanced. Pour the broth through a fine-mesh strainer into an airtight container, discarding the other ingredients. The broth will keep for up to 5 days in the refrigerator or up to 3 months in the freezer.

MAKES 3 QUARTS

Rich Mineral Broth

4 quarts water

3 (4-inch) pieces kombu

2 yellow onions, chopped

2 tablespoons extra-virgin
olive oil

2 carrots, scrubbed and chopped

1 cup dried porcini, chanterelle,
or shiitake mushrooms (or a
blend)

3 tablespoons peeled and grated
fresh ginger

1 teaspoon ground turmeric

6 sprigs thyme

2 teaspoons black peppercorns

6 dried red chiles, stemmed

1 head garlic

2 to 3 teaspoons fine-grain
sea salt

This is a simplified riff on a favorite broth from *High Vibrational Beauty* by Kerrilynn Pamer and Cindy DiPrima Morisse. It is full bodied, hearty, and versatile, with a diverse list of high-impact ingredients. Sip it or use it as the base for miso soup or to cook grains, other soups, and risottos.

Note: Miso paste is typically very salty. If you love miso soup, undersalt any broth you won't immediately use so you can repurpose the leftovers as a base for miso soup.

Add the water to a large stockpot over high heat. While the water is coming to a boil, add the kombu, onions, oil, carrots, mushrooms, ginger, turmeric, thyme, peppercorns, and chiles to the pot. Smash each garlic clove and add them to the pot. Once the broth comes to a boil, reduce the heat and simmer for 1 hour or so, until everything is very tender. Remove the pot from the heat and let it cool a bit. Pour the broth through a fine-mesh strainer into an airtight container, discarding the vegetables (or save them for another use). Taste the broth and add salt to taste. The broth will keep for up to 5 days in the refrigerator or up to 3 months in the freezer.

MAKES 3 QUARTS

White Pepper Broth

2 tablespoons extra-virgin
olive oil

2 yellow onions, halved

5 celery stalks, thinly sliced

2 carrots, scrubbed and thinly
sliced

3 tablespoons peeled and grated
fresh ginger

1 head garlic

4 quarts water, plus more as
needed

1¼ teaspoons finely ground
white pepper

2 teaspoons fine-grain sea salt,
plus more to taste

This is a monster white pepper broth, best for when the weather is at its worst or when you need to fight a cold. Add noodles, chickpeas, chopped kale, and a bit of grated cheese for an easy noodle soup.

Heat the oil in a large stockpot over medium heat. Add the onions, celery, carrots, and ginger. Smash each garlic clove and add them to the pot. Gently sauté just until soft, 4 to 5 minutes; you don't want any browning. Add a small splash of water if the pan starts to dry out. Stir in the pepper and water. Dial up the heat to bring the broth to a simmer and hold it there for 30 minutes. Remove the pot from the heat and stir in the salt. Taste and add more salt as needed. Once the broth has cooled a bit, pour it through a fine-mesh strainer into an airtight container, discarding the vegetables (or save them for another use). The broth will keep for up to 5 days in the refrigerator or up to 3 months in the freezer.

MAKES 3 QUARTS

DRESSINGS & DRIZZLES

Dressings and drizzles are the secret weapons of the culinary world, lending a nutritional boost or ingredient diversity to your dishes. They're super flexible, and you can use them over, under, or throughout whatever you're serving. If you take a foundational idea like a wrap, a salad, or a soup, a dressing or drizzle will give it a real point of view, pulling it in a strong flavor direction.

I load mine up with herbs and spices because I try to consume a range of both every day for their protective qualities and powerful phytonutrient profiles. If you keep an herb-packed, premade dressing or oil on hand, it's easy to deploy at the last minute without much thought or added preparation. Use these versions as a starting point and play around with different spice and herb blends on your own.

Boosted Avocado Dressing

½ ripe avocado

1 cup almond or oat milk, plus more to thin

1 cup spinach

1½ tablespoons thyme or oregano leaves

3 cloves garlic

1 teaspoon miso

1 tablespoon freshly squeezed lemon juice, plus more to taste

Fine-grain sea salt

Serve this up alongside a crudité platter of vibrant, crunchy vegetables. If you happen to keep spinach in the freezer for smoothies—use it here! I usually thaw it first. If you don't have miso, just salt to taste instead.

Combine the avocado, milk, spinach, thyme, garlic, miso, and lemon juice in a blender and pulse until smooth. Thin with more milk as needed to make the dressing pourable. Taste and add more lemon juice and/or salt as needed. Pour the dressing into a jar with a lid and store in the refrigerator for up to 2 days.

MAKES 2 CUPS

Magic Green Herby Drizzle

¼ cup oregano or marjoram leaves

¼ cup fresh flat-leaf parsley leaves

2 cloves garlic

½ cup extra-virgin olive oil

Pinch of fine-grain sea salt, plus more to taste

A simple garlicky green herb oil, I use this more than just about any other accent or drizzle in my cooking. Don't hold back; use it on soups or risotto or turn it into a salad dressing by adding a splash of lemon juice or white wine vinegar to taste.

In a wide-mouth jar with a lid, combine the oregano, parsley, garlic, and oil. Use a hand blender to blend until smooth. Season with salt, taste, and add more salt as needed. Store the drizzle in the refrigerator for up to a week.

MAKES ⅔ CUP

Orange & Tahini Dressing

Juice and zest of 2 oranges

3 tablespoons tahini

¼ cup extra-virgin olive oil

¼ cup chopped cilantro leaves

1 tablespoon nutritional yeast

Scant ½ teaspoon fine-grain
sea salt

In this all-purpose dressing, tahini delivers silky creaminess, while orange juice brightens and sweetens. Serve this on a salad, over simply cooked vegetables, or with noodles.

In a wide-mouth jar with a lid, whisk together the orange juice and zest, tahini, oil, cilantro, yeast, and salt. Store the dressing in the refrigerator for up to a week.

MAKES ⅔ CUP

Shallot Oil

1 cup sunflower oil or extra-virgin
olive oil

1 cup very, very thinly sliced
shallots

This is one of my favorite oils to use in a simple vinaigrette, and it's the magic touch when used on just about any lettuce greens or drizzled over ramen. Once you make the oil, you can also sprinkle the crisped shallots in salads or over anything that needs a bit of oniony crunch.

Place the oil and shallots in a thick-bottomed saucepan over medium heat. Cook the shallots slowly until deeply, deeply golden, 20 minutes or so. Remove the pan from the heat, fish out the shallots with a strainer, and place them on a paper towel to cool and crisp up. When the oil is cool, carefully transfer it to a jar with a lid. Store the oil in the refrigerator for up to 2 weeks.

MAKES I CUP

Smoked Paprika & Sumac Dressing

1 tablespoon sumac

½ teaspoon smoked paprika

Scant ¾ teaspoon fine-grain
sea salt

2 tablespoons freshly squeezed
lemon juice

1 tablespoon honey or pure
maple syrup

⅓ cup extra-virgin olive oil

Sumac is worth seeking out. It can be found in spice shops or Mediterranean and Middle Eastern markets. It's crimson colored and delightfully tangy. Drizzle this over the Summer Tomato & Celery Salad (page 92).

In a wide-mouth jar with a lid, combine the sumac, smoked paprika, salt, lemon juice, and honey. Gradually whisk in the oil. Taste and add more salt or sweetener as needed. Store the dressing in the refrigerator for up to a week.

MAKES ABOUT ½ CUP

Spicy, Crunchy Turmeric Oil

2-inch piece fresh ginger, peeled and grated

1 teaspoon ground turmeric

1½ tablespoons sesame seeds

1½ tablespoons hemp seeds

2 tablespoons crushed red pepper flakes

2 tablespoons hot paprika

2 tablespoons toasted sesame oil

6 tablespoons sunflower oil

2 tablespoons sake (optional)

1 tablespoon dark brown cane sugar

2 tablespoons white or chickpea miso

This spicy drizzle adds heat and crunch to soups and stews, noodles, hearty salads, and roasted cruciferous vegetables. I use (organic) sunflower oil because it has a neutral flavor, but substituting olive oil would, of course, be fine.

In a small saucepan over low heat, combine the ginger, turmeric, sesame and hemp seeds, red pepper flakes, paprika, and sesame and sunflower oils. Bring the mixture barely to a simmer and stir constantly for 1 minute. Remove the pan from the heat and add the sake, sugar, and miso. Return the pan to low heat and let the flavors combine, stirring constantly, for 30 seconds more. Remove the pan from the heat and let the drizzle cool. Pour it into a jar with a lid and store in the refrigerator for up to 3 weeks.

MAKES ¾ CUP

Strong Tahini-Paprika Dressing

¼ cup tahini, plus more to taste

2 tablespoons tamari, soy sauce, or coconut aminos, plus more to taste

3 tablespoons apple cider vinegar

¼ cup extra-virgin olive oil

2 small cloves garlic, smashed into a paste

1 teaspoon smoked paprika

½ teaspoon ground coriander

Scant tablespoon of honey, plus more to taste

As with the Turmeric-Almond Dressing (opposite page), this dressing is good in the way that a flavorful Japanese sesame dressing is good, served over asparagus, broccoli, or structured lettuces.

In a wide-mouth jar with a lid, whisk together the tahini, tamari, vinegar, oil, garlic, paprika, coriander, and honey. Let the dressing sit for 10 minutes, then taste, and add more tamari and/or honey as needed. Store the dressing in the refrigerator for up to a week.

MAKES ⅔ CUP

Turmeric-Almond Dressing

3-inch piece fresh turmeric, peeled, or scant ½ teaspoon ground turmeric

1 serrano chile, stemmed and seeded

1 shallot

2 cloves garlic

¼ cup whole almonds

2 tablespoons apple cider vinegar, plus more to taste

⅓ cup extra-virgin olive oil

1 tablespoon nutritional yeast

⅛ teaspoon fine-grain sea salt, plus more to taste

1 small pitted date (optional)

Stir this hearty and substantial mixture into yogurt and use it as a sandwich spread. It's also delicious as a dressing on sautéed asparagus, steamed broccoli, or sturdy lettuce salads.

Combine the turmeric, chile, shallot, garlic, almonds, vinegar, oil, yeast, and salt in a food processor fitted with a standard blade and pulse until uniform and somewhat smooth. The almonds make it tricky to get this dressing completely smooth.

Let it sit for a few minutes, then taste, and add more salt or vinegar as needed. If you like a hint of sweet to balance everything out, add the date and pulse until smooth. Pour the dressing into a jar with a lid and store in the refrigerator for up to a week.

MAKES ABOUT I CUP

NUT & SEED BUTTERS

Many people enjoy a handful of nuts or a spoonful of nut butter as a snack—myself included. But I also like to boost mine. It's an easy way to work more antioxidant- and phytonutrient-rich ingredients and whole-food powders into your everyday snacking.

Don't limit yourself once you've whipped up a jar of these butters. Once you have some on hand, there are a number of ways to eat and cook with them. The most obvious is to consume them straight or as a spread on whole grain toast, slabs of banana bread, and the like. But you can also experiment with incorporating them into sauces, dressings, or baked recipes that call for nut or seed butter.

For example, use the Five Spice Peanut Butter (page 254) in the Spicy, Creamy, Carroty Peanut Noodles (page 133) or in the California Blender Cookies (page 213). Or make simple energy bites using boosted nut or seed butters as the base. Just add instant oats or quinoa flakes, a little bit at a time, to your nut or seed butter. Keep adding and stirring until the mixture holds together. Maybe you'd like to sweeten it with some maple syrup? Go for it. Form the mixture into small balls for easy on-the-go snacks.

Berry & Pomegranate Sunflower Butter

1 tablespoon pomegranate powder

1 tablespoon goji powder

1 tablespoon raspberry or another berry powder

½ cup sunflower seed butter or 1 cup sunflower seeds

Pinch of fine-grain sea salt, plus more to taste

Pure maple syrup, honey, or coconut nectar, to taste

This tangy, vibrant seed butter combines three fruity powders into a rich spread you can use on toast, on brown rice cakes, or by the spoonful. Some of the more esoteric fruit and berry powders can be expensive, so use this recipe as a jumping-off point and mix in 3 tablespoons of whatever combination of powders you like. Freeze-dried strawberries and raspberries are increasingly available, and you can easily crush them into powders by smashing them in the bag or by rolling over the bag with a rolling pin.

If your powders are at all lumpy, sift them into a wide-mouthed jar along with the sunflower seed butter. Alternately, if you're using sunflower seeds, process them in a food processor or blender until smooth, then add the powders and process again until smooth. Add the salt and maple syrup and stir to combine. Taste and add more salt and/or sweetener as needed. Store the butter in a cool, dark place for up to a month.

MAKES ⅔ CUP

Chyawanprash Almond Butter

½ cup almond butter

2 tablespoons chyawanprash

Chyawanprash, also sometimes simply called prash, is a sticky, potent, and wonderful-tasting Ayurvedic paste made with a wild blend of herbs, honey, spices, and roots. It's a combination of ingredients that I'd never be able to combine on my own, so I source it either from Lotus Blooming Herbs or Sun Potion; see Resources (page 266). It's absolutely worth seeking out.

In a small bowl, stir together the almond butter and chyawanprash until smooth. Alternately, use a food processor or blender to combine 1 cup raw almonds with the chyawanprash and blend until smooth. Store the butter in an airtight container in a cool, dark place for up to a month.

MAKES ABOUT ⅔ CUP

Fire Butter

1 pound toasted walnuts, almonds, or hazelnuts

1 tablespoon ground cinnamon

1 teaspoon cayenne pepper

2 teaspoons ground ginger

1 tablespoon vanilla extract

2 teaspoons maca powder (optional)

1 tablespoon mesquite flour (optional)

I call this fire butter, but that's probably being overly dramatic. I love to use this spicy paste on noodles (thinned out a bit with the pasta water), on toasted walnut sourdough bread, or as part of a crudité spread with celery, carrots, and the like. Walnuts are my favorite nut for this recipe, but almonds or hazelnuts are delicious, too. You get bonus points for toasting the nuts ahead of time, but it's not necessary. There are two optional wild card ingredients: maca powder and mesquite flour. Maca is subtly nutty with butterscotch notes. It contains a whole range of vitamins and nutrients and is celebrated for increasing strength and stamina. Nutrient-rich mesquite flour has a distinct scent of malt and smoke. Along with this butter, you can use mesquite flour in baked goods and smoothies.

Combine the walnuts, cinnamon, cayenne, ginger, vanilla, maca, and flour in a food processor or blender. Process for a minute or two, until the nuts crumble and then work themselves into a paste. Store the butter in an airtight container in a cool, dark place for up to a month.

MAKES ABOUT 2 CUPS

Omega Seed Spread

½ pound raw pumpkin seeds (pepitas)

½ pound raw or toasted walnuts

½ teaspoon fine-grain sea salt

¼ cup extra-virgin olive oil or tahini, plus more as needed

2 tablespoons hemp hearts

2 tablespoons sesame seeds

1 tablespoon ground flax seeds

This pepita spread incorporates a trio of heart-healthy nuts and seeds rich in omega-3s: flax seeds, hemp hearts (from hemp seeds), and walnuts. It's great lightly slathered on hot tortillas as a base for taco ingredients. And I love to make a version using lemon olive oil for a sunny element.

Combine the pepitas, walnuts, and salt in a food processor or blender. Process for a minute or two, until the nuts crumble into a powder. While the processor is running, drizzle in the oil and process, scraping the sides of the bowl four or five times along the way, until everything comes together into a paste, 4 to 5 minutes (it can be stubborn, so you might need to blend longer than other nut butters or add a bit more oil). Transfer the blend to a bowl and stir in the hemp hearts, sesame seeds, and flax seeds. Store the butter in an airtight container in a cool, dark place for up to a month.

MAKES ABOUT 2 CUPS

Five Spice Peanut Butter

1 pound toasted unsalted peanuts

¼ teaspoon ground turmeric

½ teaspoon freshly ground black pepper

1 teaspoon ground ginger

¼ teaspoon ground cloves

2 teaspoons ground cinnamon

½ teaspoon fine-grain sea salt

1½ tablespoons pure maple syrup, dark brown cane sugar, or coconut sugar

1 tablespoon extra-virgin olive oil or coconut oil

Loaded with beneficial spices like turmeric, black pepper, and cinnamon, this butter can be used as a spread or to add a twist to your favorite peanut butter recipes; for example, Spicy, Creamy, Carroty Peanut Noodles (page 133) or California Blender Cookies (page 213).

Combine the peanuts, turmeric, pepper, ginger, cloves, cinnamon, salt, and maple syrup in a food processor or blender. Process for a minute or two, until the nuts crumble and then work themselves into a paste. Add the oil and process for another minute, until the butter is fluffy and light. Store the butter in an airtight container in a cool, dark place for up to a month.

MAKES ABOUT 2 CUPS

PASTES

These pastes are great ways to incorporate more herbs, spices, and beneficial ingredients like miso into your cooking. They also provide a quick flavor-packed base for soups, stews, stir-fries, and curries. Stir a tablespoon of paste into just about any savory dish and see what happens. Coconut milk, casseroles, savory pie or tart fillings, pots of rice, and noodle bowls are all fair game. Or smash a dollop into a bowl of ripe avocado with a bit of citrus zest and a pinch of salt for a twist on guacamole.

Keeping power pastes on hand is one of my favorite weeknight shortcuts, and I prefer homemade pastes to store-bought ones, despite the extra effort involved. Beyond the nutritional benefits, making your own pastes allows you to completely customize the strength of flavors, degree of spiciness, and freshness of ingredients. Your family loves ginger? Try doubling down on it. Doesn't love cumin? Try a spice they prefer.

These recipes make generous batches. Store as much as you might use in a week in the refrigerator and freeze the rest, flat, in small resealable plastic bags or ice cube trays.

California Tom Yum Paste

4 shallots, peeled and quartered

3 stalks lemongrass, trimmed and tender centers coarsely chopped

2 serrano chiles, seeded

2 quarter-size slices fresh ginger, peeled and coarsely chopped

4 makrut lime leaves, torn and smashed

Zest of 1 Meyer lemon (optional)

½ teaspoon fine-grain sea salt

We have an abundance of Meyer lemons in California and I like to use them in this vegetarian take on tom yum paste. Fiercely aromatic with shallots playing alongside generous amounts of ginger and chile, this paste banks into citrus territory with the trifecta of lemongrass, Meyer lemon, and makrut lime. Try it slathered inside spring rolls, spread across flatbreads, or whisked into Greek yogurt. Make a double batch and freeze what you don't immediately use for up to 3 months.

Using a mortar and pestle, smash the shallots, lemongrass, chiles, ginger, lime leaves, lemon zest, and salt into a very rough paste. (If your mortar and pestle is on the small size, work in batches or pulse into a paste in a food processor.) Store the paste in an airtight container in the refrigerator for up to a week.

MAKES ⅔ CUP

Cilantro–Green Curry Paste

2-inch piece fresh ginger, peeled

4 shallots

Generous bunch cilantro

6 cloves garlic

3 serrano chiles, seeded

3 green onions, white and green parts

1 teaspoon ground turmeric

1 teaspoon crushed red pepper flakes

3 tablespoons coconut cream

¼ teaspoon fine-grain sea salt, plus more to taste

One of my most used pastes, this is heavy on cilantro and ginger, with a good dose of turmeric. It can be subbed in just about any recipe that calls for green curry paste. Use the cream from the top of a can of full-fat coconut milk here.

In a food processor or blender, combine the ginger, shallots, cilantro, garlic, chiles, green onions, turmeric, red pepper flakes, coconut cream, and salt. Pulse until the mixture forms a paste. Taste and add more salt as needed. Store the paste in an airtight container in the refrigerator for up to a week or freeze for up to 3 months.

MAKES 1½ CUPS

Miso Ramen Paste

4 green onions, white and tender green parts, thinly sliced

3-inch piece fresh ginger, peeled and grated

4 cloves garlic, grated

2 tablespoons mirin

1 tablespoon fermented gochujang paste, curry paste, or sriracha

1 cup white miso or chickpea miso (see Note)

1 teaspoon crushed red pepper flakes

2 teaspoons nutritional yeast

Think of this as the seasoning paste for your ramen broth. You can also add hot water and use it for spice-charged miso soup. You might even whisk a bit into a favorite dressing. Other things you can certainly add to this paste: a bit of ground turmeric, chopped cilantro or basil, or crushed sesame seeds.

Note: If you are avoiding soy, seek out chickpea or other non-soy miso.

In a small saucepan over low heat, combine the green onions, ginger, garlic, mirin, gochujang paste, miso, and red pepper flakes. You just want to warm this for 2 to 3 minutes, until the ginger, garlic, and green onions sweat a bit. Remove the pan from the heat and stir in the yeast. Store the paste in an airtight container in the refrigerator for up to a week or freeze for up to 3 months.

MAKES 1¼ CUPS

Turmeric-Lemongrass Paste

4 lemongrass stalks, trimmed and tender centers coarsely chopped

6 cloves garlic

6 shallots

3 serrano chiles, seeded

3-inch piece fresh ginger, peeled

1½ teaspoons ground cumin

2 teaspoons ground turmeric

¼ cup extra-virgin coconut or olive oil, or sunflower oil

Drizzle of lime oil or zest of 1 lime (optional)

My go-to yellow curry paste, this has an assertive lineup of turmeric, ginger, chiles, cumin, and other aromatics. To prepare lemongrass, remember that you're after the tender part in the center of each stalk. Peel the fibrous layers back and discard. Trim any tough parts at the top and tail. If you think your turmeric might be less than premium (which can make it bitter and acrid), start with less than what is called for and add more to taste.

In a mortar and pestle, smash the lemongrass, then add the garlic, shallots, chiles, ginger, cumin, and turmeric one at a time, mashing after each addition. Alternately, you can pulse in a food processor or blender until the ingredients start to come together. Add the coconut oil and blend again. Stir in the lime oil. Store the paste in an airtight container in the refrigerator for up to a week or freeze for up to 3 months.

MAKES 1½ CUPS

Winter Green Miso Paste

½ cup miso

⅔ cup extra-virgin olive oil

4 cloves garlic

1½ tablespoons fresh rosemary

1 large bunch cilantro

16 green onions, white and tender green parts

2-inch piece fresh ginger, peeled

This rosemary-scented miso paste is the base of Winter Green Miso Soup (page 116), but it's also right at home tossed with soba noodles or even slathered across flatbread dough (see page 162) and topped with lots of vegetables for a quick dinner.

In a food processor or blender, combine the miso, oil, garlic, rosemary, cilantro, green onions, and ginger and puree into a green-flecked paste. Store the paste in an airtight container in the refrigerator for up to a week or freeze for up to 3 months.

MAKES 2 CUPS

WHOLE GRAIN BLENDS

Whole grains are powerful health promoters, and you see them as a component of nearly every traditional diet that's celebrated for longevity rates. When you limit your diet to refined grains or products made from them (like white bread or white rice), you're missing out on a whole host of vitamins, nutrients, and minerals that get stripped out. Whole grains like oats, barley, whole grain rice, quinoa, or wheat berries are known to help reduce some of the scariest health issues we face—everything from hypertension and heart disease to diabetes, cancer, and osteoporosis. They're also delicious, filling, and incredibly adaptable.

Thankfully, there is a wonderful spectrum of whole grains available to us. Combining them into powerful blends, along with other pulses, seeds, and spices, is a great way to become familiar with the range of options. Cook up a pot of grains once or twice a week and you'll have all sorts of menu possibilities. Cooking grains at home is also more economical than buying precooked rice and grains. Use them as the foundation for a bowl or the filling for a wrap. Thinned out with broth, they make wonderful porridges, soups, or risotto-style meals. Experimenting with *blends* of whole grains allows you to get a bigger variety of nutrients in each meal because each grain is unique. This section highlights a number of my stand-out blends. Although I like to revisit these often, dreaming up and then experimenting with new ideas is part of the fun. Play around!

Note: I have you soak all of the blends for at least 20 minutes, but if you can soak them longer, preferably overnight in the refrigerator, the nutrients are more bio-available and the grains more easily digestible.

Almond Porridge Blend

1 cup brown basmati rice

½ cup buckwheat groats

¼ cup quinoa

¼ cup millet

2 cups water

1¾ cups almond milk

1½ teaspoons fine-grain sea salt

1 tablespoon ghee or extra-virgin olive oil

1 teaspoon crushed caraway seeds

½ teaspoon crushed red pepper flakes

Pinch of saffron

⅓ cup toasted sliced almonds

The nuttiness of basmati rice combined with almond accents is what makes this blend special. It's a nice porridge base that goes well with spices, cooked fruit, and bright berries.

Combine the rice, buckwheat, quinoa, and millet in a fine-mesh strainer. Rinse and transfer the grains to a medium saucepan. Add the water, milk, and salt and soak for at least 20 minutes or overnight in the refrigerator (if you have the time).

Once soaked, add the ghee, caraway seeds, red pepper flakes, and saffron. Bring to a boil over medium-high heat, then dial back the heat and simmer gently, covered, for 35 to 40 minutes, until the water has been absorbed and the ingredients are cooked through. Fluff the grains with a fork and remove the pan from the heat. Let the grains sit, covered, for another 10 minutes before serving topped with the almonds.

SERVES 6

Basmati Rice & Lentils

1⅓ cups brown basmati rice

⅓ cup French lentils (lentilles du Puy)

⅓ cup blended quinoa, hato mugi (Job's tears), and/or millet

3¾ cups water or vegetable broth

½ teaspoon fine-grain sea salt

This is a blend I make often, using small amounts of any quick-cooking grains I have on hand, typically French lentils (lentilles du Puy), quinoa, millet, or hato mugi (Job's tears), a favorite of mine. Job's tears are chubby, teardrop-shaped whole grains that have been celebrated in Asian cultures for centuries and are wonderfully chewy when cooked.

Combine the rice, lentils, and other grains in a fine-mesh strainer. Rinse and transfer the grains to a medium saucepan. Add the water and salt and soak for at least 20 minutes or overnight in the refrigerator (if you have the time). Once soaked, bring the grains to a boil over medium-high heat, then dial back the heat and gently simmer, covered, for 35 to 40 minutes, until the water has been absorbed and the ingredients are cooked through. Fluff the grains with a fork and remove the pan from the heat. Let the grains sit, covered, for another 10 minutes before serving.

SERVES 6

Blackout Beans & Rice

1½ cups black rice

¼ cup adzuki beans

¼ cup black beluga lentils

2 tablespoons black sesame seeds

3¼ cups water or Black Garlic Broth (page 241)

1 cup well-mixed, full-fat coconut milk

¾ teaspoon fine-grain sea salt

This dish is a creamy, sesame-flecked version of one-pot beans and rice. I like this as a component in homemade burritos or as a base for black onigiri (Japanese rice triangles; see page 180).

Combine the rice, beans, lentils, and sesame seeds in a fine-mesh strainer. Rinse and transfer the grains to a medium saucepan. Add the water and soak for at least 20 minutes or overnight in the refrigerator (if you have the time). Once soaked, add the coconut milk and salt. Bring to a boil over medium-high heat, then dial back the heat and simmer gently, covered, for 50 to 60 minutes, until the water has been absorbed and the ingredients are cooked through. Fluff the grains with a fork and remove the pan from the heat. Let the grains sit, covered, for another 10 minutes before serving.

SERVES 6

Purple Jasmine, Seeds & Spices

1½ cups purple jasmine rice

¼ cup buckwheat groats

¼ cup black beluga lentils or French lentils (lentilles du Puy)

3 cups water or vegetable broth

1 teaspoon fine-grain sea salt

3 tablespoons sunflower seeds

3 tablespoons raw pumpkin seeds (pepitas)

1 teaspoon whole coriander seeds, crushed a bit

1 teaspoon whole cumin seeds

1 teaspoon crushed red pepper flakes

1 cup well-mixed, full-fat coconut milk

1 tablespoon flax seeds, crushed, to serve

Punctuated with seeds and peppered with spices, this is a maximalist rice blend. If you're trying to work more seeds and spices into your diet, this does some of the work for you. To take things over the top, drizzle with Shallot Oil (see page 247) and sprinkle with shallot crisps to serve.

Combine the rice, buckwheat, and lentils in a fine-mesh strainer. Rinse and transfer the grains to a medium saucepan. Add the water and salt and soak for at least 20 minutes or overnight in the refrigerator (if you have the time). Once soaked, add the sunflower seeds, pepitas, coriander seeds, cumin seeds, red pepper flakes, and coconut milk. Bring to a boil over medium-high heat, then dial back the heat and gently simmer, covered, for 40 to 45 minutes, until the water has been absorbed and the ingredients are cooked through. Fluff the grains with a fork and remove the pan from the heat.

Let the grains sit, covered, for another 10 minutes before serving, topped with the flax seeds.

SERVES 6

Pink Himalayan Mushroom Rice

2 cups pink Himalayan rice

3½ cups Favorite Mushroom Broth (page 242)

½ cup well-mixed, full-fat coconut milk

½ teaspoon pink Himalayan salt

Blushing rose-hued grains of rice simmer in flavorful mushroom broth, enriched with a hit of coconut milk, resulting in a fantastic base for any grain bowl, wrap, or even onigiri (Japanese rice triangles; see page 180). This dish is a nice example of how to experiment with all the beautiful rice varieties now available.

Rinse the rice in a fine-mesh strainer, then transfer to a medium saucepan and add the broth, coconut milk, and salt. Soak for at least 20 minutes or overnight in the refrigerator (if you have the time). Once soaked, bring to a boil over medium-high heat, then dial back the heat and simmer gently, covered, for 40 to 50 minutes, until the broth has been absorbed. Fluff the grains with a fork and remove the pan from the heat. Let the grains sit, covered, for another 10 minutes before serving.

SERVES 6

Sesame Brown Rice

2 cups short-grain brown rice

3¾ cups water or vegetable broth

½ teaspoon fine-grain sea salt

1 tablespoon toasted sesame oil

2 tablespoons white or black sesame seeds, plus more to serve

Sliced green onions, white and tender green parts, and lemon zest, to serve (optional)

You can use white or black sesame seeds here or even a mix. Black seeds will lend a dark tint to the rice, whereas white seeds won't. Omit the sesame oil and sesame seeds for a great basic pot of brown rice and use any leftovers for Grilled Rice Triangles (page 180).

Rinse the rice in a fine-mesh strainer, then transfer to a medium saucepan and add the water, salt, sesame oil, and sesame seeds. Soak for at least 20 minutes or overnight in the refrigerator (if you have the time). Once soaked, bring to a boil over medium-high heat, then dial back the heat and simmer, covered, for 40 to 50 minutes, until the water has been absorbed. Fluff the rice with a fork and remove the pan from the heat. Let the rice sit, covered, for another 10 minutes before serving topped with more sesame seeds, green onions, and lemon zest.

SERVES 6

Resources

ASSORTED INGREDIENTS

Big Tree Farms
Coconut aminos and coconut
palm sugars and nectar.
bigtreefarms.com

Brightland
Single-estate, California extra-virgin
olive oil, packaged in UV-protected
glass, plus lemon oil and red chile oil.
brightland.co

Eden Foods
Wide range of organic products.
edenfoods.com

Guittard Chocolate
San Francisco–based, family-run
chocolate company.
guittard.com

Hudson
Titi's Extra Virgin Olive Oil, estate grown
and made from Tuscan varietal olive trees
in Northern California.
hudsonranch.com

Just Date Syrup
Date syrup made from organic California dates
and the first organic and refined sugar–free
pomegranate syrup.
justdatesyrup.com

Katz
Family-owned, California-based company;
variety of artisan vinegars (the Late Harvest
Sauvignon Blanc Vinegar is a staple).
katzfarm.com

Lotus Foods
Organic, fair-trade, and heirloom rice
and rice noodles.
lotusfoods.com

Toiro
Impeccably sourced Japanese pantry items
and traditional donabe cooking vessels.
toirokitchen.com

Trader Joe's
Whole wheat pizza dough, candied hibiscus
flowers, frozen artichoke hearts, and nuts
and seeds.
traderjoes.com

Wonder Valley
Extra-virgin olive oil made from Northern California
olives and packaged in UV-protected glass.
welcometowondervalley.com

FLOURS, GRAINS, PASTA & PULSES

Alter Eco
Organic, fair trade, and heirloom quinoa.
alterecofoods.com

Anson Mills
Organic heirloom grains.
ansonmills.com

Arrowhead Mills
Organic beans, grains, and seeds.
arrowheadmills.com

Banza
Chickpea pasta.
eatbanza.com

Hayden Flour Mills
Family-owned company; heritage grains and flours.
haydenflourmills.com

Le Sanctuaire
Herbs, spices, flowers, seeds, salts, and spice blends, including my favorite shichimi togarashi.
le-sanctuaire.mybigcommerce.com

Massa Organics
Family-owned, California-based company; organic brown rice, almonds, and almond butter.
massaorganics.com

Rancho Gordo
Heirloom beans and new-world grains and seeds.
ranchogordo.com

Taste Republic
Gluten-free, grain-free fresh pasta.
tasterepublicglutenfree.com

SEASONINGS, SPICES, POWDERS & CONDIMENTS

Aedan Fermented Foods
Small-batch organic miso, koji, and amazake.
aedansf.com

Alteya Organics
Food-grade Bulgarian rose water.
alteyaorganics.com

CAP Beauty
Whole-food powders and adaptogens.
capbeauty.com

Diaspora Co.
Organic turmeric, chiles, and other spices.
diasporaco.com

Dr. Cowan's Garden
Whole-food vegetable powders.
drcowansgarden.com

Halen Mon
Oak-smoked sea salt and demerara sugar.
halenmon.com

Lotus Blooming Herbs
Chyawanprash jam.
lotusbloomingherbs.com

Mike's Organic Foods
High-quality organic curry pastes made in Thailand and Sri Lanka.
mikesorganicfoods.com

Mountain Rose Herbs
Organic herbs, spices, flowers, pollens, and powders.
mountainroseherbs.com

Navitas Organics
Organic seeds, powders, goji berries, and cacao.
navitasorganics.com

South River Miso Company
Traditional, wood-fired, unpasteurized, organic misos.
southrivermiso.com

Sun Potion
Adaptogens, mushroom powders, matcha, chyawanprash, and honey.
sunpotion.com

HOUSEWARES, EQUIPMENT & TABLETOP ITEMS

Block Shop
Los Angeles–based company; handmade textiles.
blockshoptextiles.com

Cloutier Ceramics
Small-batch ceramics made in Northern California.
cloutierceramics.com

Colleen Hennessey Clayworks
Hand-thrown, high-fired ceramics made in Mendocino, California.
colleenhennessey.net

deVOL
Ceramic tableware, brass knobs and rails, stand-alone cupboards, and curated vintage items.
devolkitchens.com

Food52
Expansive culinary emporium, content, and community.
food52.com

GARDE
High-end tabletop items and ceramics from small producers and artisans.
gardeshop.com

General Store
California-based lifestyle shop with ceramics, textiles, and kitchen items.
shop-generalstore.com

Goodwill
I haunt them wherever I travel for unique glassware and plates.
goodwill.org

Heath Ceramics
Ceramic tableware made in Sausalito and San Francisco, plus a wide range of other culinary-realm producers.
heathceramics.com

Herriott Grace
Curated father-daughter culinary shop with one-of-a-kind hand-carved wood spoons and pedestals and small-batch porcelain and stoneware.
herriottgrace.com

Jacob May Design
Made-in-California cutting boards, tables, and countertops.
jacob-may.com

Malinda Reich
One-of-a-kind wheel-thrown and hand-carved ceramics made in San Francisco.
malindareich.com

MARCH
High-end culinary items from a broad range of artisan producers.
marchsf.com

Marian Bull
Color-forward, one-of-a-kind ceramics made in Brooklyn.
bullinachinashop.info

Nickey Kehoe

Los Angeles–based company; home
furnishings, ceramics, tabletop items,
linens, and vintage.
nickeykehoe.com

Permanent Collection

Heritage-quality culinary items: hand-turned
redwood bowls, stoneware, and hand-forged
spoons.
permanentcollection.com

Sarah Kersten

Fermentation crocks, plates, platters,
and vases made in Northern California.
sarahkersten.com

Thank You

This is the first cookbook I've written and photographed while living away from San Francisco, the city I consider home. It's where my family is, where my publisher is, where I've had many of my formative experiences, and where I know the stores, markets, and purveyors like the back of my hand. Part of the reason our transition to Los Angeles has been smoother than expected was the support of all the individuals mentioned here, along with a steady stream of visitors for me to test recipes on and share meals with. We joke that we had more houseguests in our first year in Los Angeles than in the last ten years in San Francisco, and it was a great way to put some of these recipes through their paces.

Wayne Bremser: For always keeping the wheels on the bus.

My Ten Speed family: Although I miss being able to pop over to the office, I couldn't ask for a better experience taking my books from start to finish. Julie Bennett, I can't believe this is our fourth (nearly fifteen years!). Thanks for being a steady hand, guiding force, and all-around great editor. To Annie Marino for taking these color-soaked Southern California photos and recipes and pulling them together with a beautiful book design. Aaron Wehner, Lorena Jones, Serena Sigona, and everyone at Ten Speed Press, thank you.

There are many people who inspired, contributed to, or helped in the making of this book: Gary Swanson, Janelle Swanson, Heather, Jack & Mark Ruder, Malinda Reich, Bonni Evensen, Chanda Williams, Aran Goyoaga, Deborah Williamson, Andrea Gentl, Souris Hong & JP Bernbach, Brian Hickman, Steve Sando, Leah Rosenberg, Colleen Hennessey, Naoko Takei Moore, Heidi Merrick, Lily & Hopie Stockman, Sarah Kersten, Kerrilyn Pamer, and Cindy DiPrima Morisse.

And deepest thanks to all of you who have cooked from my books or invited my recipes into your own kitchens. Nothing makes me happier than seeing photos of your well-worn, spattered, and stained copies of *Super Natural Cooking*, *Near & Far*, or *Super Natural Every Day*.

Index

All rights reserved.
Published in the United States by Ten Speed Press, an imprint of
Random House, a division of Penguin Random House LLC, New York.
www.tenspeed.com

Ten Speed Press and the Ten Speed Press colophon are registered
trademarks of Penguin Random House LLC.

All photographs are by Heidi Swanson with the exception of the
following: page 2 by Wayne Bremser.

Library of Congress Cataloging-in-Publication Data
    Names: Swanson, Heidi, 1973- author.
    Title: Super natural simple : whole-food, vegetarian recipes
        for real life / Heidi Swanson.
    Description: First editon. | California : Ten Speed Press, [2021] |
        Includes index.
    Identifiers: LCCN 2020011816 (print) | LCCN 2020011817 (ebook)
        | ISBN 9781984856883 (trade paperback) | ISBN
        9781984856890 (ebook)
    Subjects: LCSH: Cooking (Natural foods) | Vegetarian cooking. |
        Quick and easy cooking. | LCGFT: Cookbooks.
    Classification: LCC TX741 .S8876 2021 (print) | LCC TX741 (ebook) |
        DDC 641.5/636—dc23
        LC record available at https://lccn.loc.gov/2020011816
        LC ebook record available at https://lccn.loc.gov/2020011817

Trade Paperback ISBN: 978-1-9848-5688-3
eBook ISBN: 978-1-9848-5689-0

Printed in China

Editor: Julie Bennett
Designer: Annie Marino
Production designers: Mari Gill and Mara Gendell
Production manager: Serena Sigona
Prepress color manager: Jane Chinn
Food and prop stylist: Heidi Swanson
Copyeditor: Dolores York
Proofreader: Linda Bouchard
Indexer: Ken DellaPenta
Publicist: Kristin Casemore
Marketer: Daniel Wikey

10 9 8 7 6 5 4 3 2 1

First Edition